As one who spent my school holidays y
Kerala village, this book took me back about 60 years in time. Our village had no electricity until 1966, but life amid the ponds, the mango, coconut and cashew groves, the games played between sugarcane and paddy fields were full of charm. Elders took us to temple festivals in buses that broke down and nobody complained because passengers would get chatting. There was intrigue and familiarity when the postman did much more than deliver letters. Workmen were forever doing something around the house, which always had visitors. A bullock cart with loudspeakers came by advertising the new cinema in town ... all of this and more reappear colourfully in these delightful memories of K T Rajagopalan. Loosely linked, these 30 true, heartwarming, witty slice-of-life stories are all written in the compelling style of fine fiction.

Mohan Sivanand, former Editor-in-Chief,
Reader's Digest India

Malabar Musings records the nostalgic thoughts about a tiny Kerala village in the 1950s. Evocative and charming, the chapters bring alive a bygone era in a delightful and gently humorous way. The book is of incalculable value for the light it throws on how Malabar (and, by extension, the rest of the country) has changed in the last seven decades. The beauty of the book lies in the fact that it does not attempt a direct comparison between then and now, but by describing incidents from his childhood in impeccable language, Rajagopalan subtly hints at the transformation that has taken place. Whether it is about his family, retainers, school, friends or life in general in Koodaali, the author's nostalgic reminiscences are an absolute joy to read. If only one could put the clock back!

Khyrunnisa A, author

It is often said that there is nothing like recalling the childhood memories to make one a better human being. In a highly complex world, getting more and more complicated as one grows old, the tendency for such a recall is compelling. Interestingly, the innocence or naiveté of that age would even be lauded as a virtue lost forever. As a seasoned blogger, translator and story-teller, Rajagopalan has perfected a style which is direct, simple, and engaging. Hence these musings are sure to take the readers down the memory lane through the feudal life of Malabar villages of the fifties.

Sethu, novelist and
former Chairman of National Book Trust

This ex-banker, who is a bibliophile, a puzzler and a cruciverbalist all rolled into one, has found his métier as a writer of rare skill ... collection of vignettes from the Malabar of the 1950s ... takes us back in time to a world that has vanished into the mists of fading memories ... a world with the wind wafting through coconut trees, and water gurgling in little streams, while children laughed on their way to school, running along perilously narrow bunds separating paddy fields, carrying only a slate and one textbook ... a world of large joint families, avuncular chefs running large kitchens, wise teachers well versed in the mysterious art of symbolism, elderly knights jousting over improvised chessboards ... deft touch in selecting anecdotes to recount ... beautiful yet economical descriptions ... anecdotal accounts that provide a glimpse into life as it was lived and experienced ... powerfully evocative images conjured up ... redolent of the smells and flavours of our childhood ...

C Balagopal, bureaucrat,
entrepreneur and author

Witty and evocative, Rajagopalan's vivid sketches of life in a rustic village in Kannur in the fifties draw word pictures of a place and a people lost in time. The delightful collection is filled with memorable people and incidents that evoke nostalgia and laughter in equal measure.

Saraswathy Nagarajan,
Deputy Editor, The Hindu

Here is a delightful collection of tales that brings alive a bygone age of Malabar. These are reflective narratives, often anecdotal in style, that linger lovingly on the strange ordinariness of characters while offering surgically acute peeks into their often quirky, innocently messy lives set amidst the paradoxes of a different milieu. Tinged with humour and empathy, captivating in visceral detailing, they paint a fragile epoch; a dappled Malabar of laughter and torment, celebrating little lives and lost longings.

Dr Meena T Pillai
Visiting Professor
Department of World Arts and Cultures
University of California, Los Angeles

MALABAR MUSINGS

Untold tales from my village

K T Rajagopalan

MALABAR MUSINGS

Untold tales from my village

Non-fiction / Memoirs

K T Rajagopalan
Sayujyam. E65 Kattachal Road
Tirumala, Thiruvananthapuram 695 006
Kerala India
ktremail@gmail.com
Phone 91 471 2353555/91 9446 070 555

Cover art and illustrations: Baburajan Muliyankeezhil
Cover design: Shirley Khaitan and Mohan Sivanand
Printing: pothi.com

My Grandfather
Keezhooridatthil Kunhiraman Vaazhunnavar
who initiated me into the world of letters

and

My grandchildren
Meera and **Maya**
who, I hope, will carry forward the torch

I do not know who paints the picture of life on the canvas called memory. Whoever she might be, it's nothing but painting. That is, she doesn't pick up brushes to make an exact copy of what's happening around. She casts away lots of things, but retains lots of others, depending on her whims. Many insignificant happenings are made bigger, and gigantic episodes scaled down. The painter doesn't hesitate to put later things in front and earlier things behind. For a fact, her task is painting pictures, not writing history.

So, on the exterior of our life, there is a procession of events, and within, pictures are drawn continuously. The two are connected, but not the same.

Rabindra Nath Tagore in *Jeeban smriti* (Memoirs)*

No one can say beforehand what among the childhood experiences will be retained, and what will be erased forever. There is no rule that tells us what we will remember and what we won't. That is the magic about memory.

Satyajit Ray in *Jokhon chhoto chhilam* (When I was a child) *

* Translations by Santanu Sinha Chaudhuri

CONTENTS

INTRODUCTION

I have a confession to make: when God made me, He had temporarily run out of his stock of imagination. Therefore, I was born without that attribute. Which explains why real stories of actual events, involving real people, populate this small volume. Barring the few instances where the characters (or their relatives) might be upset, were they to read those stories, I have retained the original names.

"When you want something, all the universe conspires in helping you to achieve it", said Paulo Coelho in *The Alchemist*. A joint conspiracy was hatched by a number of people in realising this dream of mine. For want of a better system, I choose to list the names of the conspirators chronologically.

- K Santosh, formerly of The Hindu, for discovering and encouraging the story-teller in me.
- Saraswathy Nagarajan, also of The Hindu, who kept saying, 'KTR, you can do it, you must do it'.
- My brother K T Radhakrishnan who filled in some of the details I had missed out or did not recall.
- My friends Santanu Sinha Chaudhuri, Damodar Menon, A N Jyothi and Philip

Abraham who went through the manuscripts minutely.

- Beena Vijayalakshmy, Ramdas Menon, R Ram Mohan, Sameer Parekh, Kalpana Sadasivan and Shobha Nayar-Pandit who literally pushed me into this venture and urged me to compile my writings which lay scattered at different places.
- Baburajan Muliyankeezhil who made my stories attractive through his brilliant sketches and my friend Mangad Rathnakaran who introduced me to Baburajan.
- Mohan Sivanand, former Editor-in-Chief of Readers' Digest India who used the finest toothcomb I have ever come across. He wielded his blue pencil to cut a lot of the flab and guided me, step by step, at every stage.
- Khyrunnisa A, Mani Menon, Capt Prem G Nath, R S Arora and Ritu Arora for their tips on publishing.
- Shirley Khaitan for the splendid job she did designing the front cover.
- M Varadaraja Iyer, for putting it all together in this form,
- and, last but not least, my resident editor (and wife) Bhawani Cheerath.

PROLOGUE

This book contains accounts of what I remember of my childhood spent in the non-descript village called Koodaali in what was then the Malabar District of the erstwhile British Malabar Presidency.

We were part of a large joint family staying in a large house, sharing common facilities with a few other similar houses in the village accommodating other members of the matriarchal family. Such an arrangement is inconceivable in the twenty-first century and therefore would bear some explanation.

The properties of the *Tharawaad,* the family, were administered by the *Kaaranavar,* the seniormost male member of the family. All the expenses of the members were met from the income from these properties. While the Kaaranavar lived in the main residential unit with his wife and children, members of the family – meaning his sisters and unmarried brothers as well as matrilineal cousins – were distributed in the few large houses within a furlong (200 meters) or two from the main unit.

Each unit had a kitchen, a cook and a group of menial servants. Physicians, goldsmiths, laundrymen, barbers, tailors and other service personnel were common to all houses. The Kaaranavar would supply the victuals and provisions for the kitchens. The practice was that a man who marries into the family would stay in his wife's house. Only when he became the Kaaranavar in his matrilineal family would he return to his Tharawaad.

All these are things of the past. The inexorable changes ushered in by the land reforms, the general churn in the society and the shift in the familial structure have consigned all those to the back of beyond of one's mind.

ESHMAAN'S MEDICINE

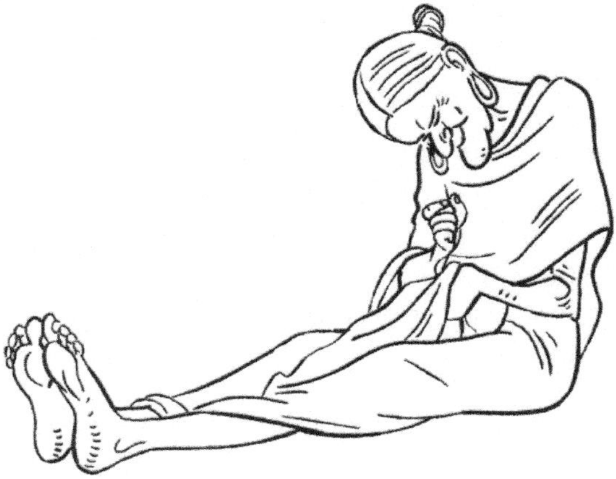

From the day I can remember (which is when I was seven), Paaru Amma was part of our family. She looked ancient, really wizened. Given her slender frame with a more than slight stoop, her toothless grin, wrinkled skin and shock of silver hair, she could not have been less than seventy then.

You could refer to her as the 'dowry' that Aunt Rema brought with her, a maid-in-waiting. When Kesava ammaaman, my maternal uncle, married his maternal uncle's daughter Rema (the done thing among many families in Kerala) and brought her home, she was accompanied by Paaru Amma. It must have been a tough decision for Janaki Amma, Aunt Rema's mother, to 'give her away in dowry': she had been part of her family for decades. Incidentally, everyone in the family addressed the old retainer with an honorific Paaru 'Amma', but, Janaki Amma and Paaru Amma were on first name terms. The Lady of the House was plain and simple Jaanu for her hand-maiden Paaru.

One of those evenings when, back from school, I was pottering about in the coconut grove with Paaru Amma, I asked her how the matronly and awe-inspiring Janaki Amma was a mere Jaanu to her. Prompt was her reply: How else do you address a classmate? Jaanu and I sat on the same bench from Class I to V.

Though everyone in the family called her Paaru Amma, she never returned the favour. She would refer to everyone, young or old, by their name, or even pet name. Thus, Kesava Ammaaman's brother was just Govi to her; my mother's uncle, then a Major in the British Army, was a mere Naanu, and his brother, a school teacher, was just Kannan. The only concession she made was in the case of Kesava Ammaaman: the man who was a mere Kesavan, got promoted to '*Eshmaan*' (the corrupt form of *Yajamaanan* – for Master) upon his marriage.

She was the first one in our home to get up and the last to go to bed; between the two events, you'd never see her resting. I do not know for sure, but I guess she sought no compensation for her services: she was happy to be part of the family. All her needs were taken care of and she seemed to have no use for money.

Paaru Amma was a great help to the family – particularly to the children, young brides and female folk. She made countless toys using local resources – palm fronds, plumeria blooms or banana stems. She would teach us swimming. She would undertake the delicate task of telling the pre-teen girls about the birds and the bees – revealing enough for their age and no more. Those preparing to get married were apprenticed to her and received good training in cuisine, housekeeping and administration. She would provide wise counsel to young brides. Mothers would go to her for advice on how to tackle their errant children.

Not much was known about her personal life – whether she was married at all or had children. In any case, she never mentioned them. I believe that Paaru Amma had no relatives – at least none that we knew of. She was at our home 24 x 365 and had nowhere else to go. That perhaps explains how she came to integrate herself with the family so very closely.

Once a postman came home with a money order for Rs 10 – a princely sum in those days – addressed to one Purakkal Parvathi Amma. There was nobody at home who answered to that name. It was Paaru Amma's formal name, but she refused the remittance. 'Return it to the sender', she told the postman. That was the only time I found her bitter about something in life. The sender may have been her long-lost husband or son; we will never know.

As age advanced, Paaru Amma bent double, lost weight (if that were indeed possible) and her health deteriorated. Aunt Rema nursed her well and she bounced back to life in no time. Towards the end, she would get blackouts: while busy doing something or talking to someone, she would just 'drop dead'. What started as infrequently as once a month gradually happened more often. One forenoon, when Aunt Rema left for her bath, she saw Paaru Amma seated on her favourite stool in the kitchen with the chopping board in her lap and dicing vegetables. When she returned, the old lady was motionless. Aunt Rema put some smelling salts to her nostrils and, slowly, Paaru Amma opened her eyes. Another day, when Aunt Rema's school-going daughter rushed in to put her empty lunch box for washing, there she was, lying on her back, ladle in hand, next to the fireplace. She let out a howl and Paaru Amma sat up! The redeeming feature was that though the interludes grew more frequent in course of time, the blackout periods became shorter.

As such episodes recurred, the local *vaidyan* (physician) suggested some Ayurvedic concoction. Though one does not know of the efficacy of this medication, she would be up and about in about ten minutes or twenty, open her eyes and smile, saying, "It's not yet time for Him to call me." During one such episode, Murali, another uncle of mine who came visiting, suggested that a bit of brandy be administered to her. In those days, households of even teetotaller families would have stock of a little of the potion – it was believed that brandy hastens the healing process of young mothers. In any case, as my uncle, the

Eshmaan, used to have an occasional drink, the stuff was readily available at home.

It worked! That done, in no time, Paaru Amma sat up and smiled beatifically. God's in his heaven, and all's right with the world!

The next time she was losing consciousness, Aunt Rema rushed to fetch the smelling salts, but Paaru Amma called out, "Rema, get me Eshmaan's medicine, not the smelling salts!"

Sad to say, she did not live long to have many more doses of Eshmaan's medicine.

SPARE THE ROD ...

Speaking of his childhood, American humorist Sam Levenson wrote something that goes like this: "Those days mothers had not heard of newfangled ideas like child psychology that could be used on erring children; they used whatever they could lay their hands on – like the ladle or the rolling pin." This was something that I had read in the 1960s while in college, but it sprang back from somewhere in the recesses of my memory the other day when I read of corporal punishment having been banned in Kerala's schools. It also transported me back to the first time I was administered such punishment.

That was 1951. I attended the only school in our village, a couple of miles from home. That was a primary school which taught up to Class V. For 'higher studies', one needed to go to the elementary school, which was almost another three miles away. After three years there, you had to go to the high school, which was even farther by a good two miles.

More than the school, all the fun was in the saunter to school and back. You had to foot it all the way, whether you crossed the paddy fields or took the dirt track up and down the hillock and then through the motorable village road. The paddy route was a shortcut and less arduous because the terrain was plain. It was great fun negotiating the fragile ribbon-like ridges that separated neighbouring fields.

With a slate and the only (yes, we had just one!) textbook in one hand and lunch packed in plantain leaf in the other, Bhaskaran, Rasheed, Sarojini, Ananthan and I would walk along the ridge, in single file, to the school and back, stopping *en route* to make friends with frogs and grasshoppers, dragonflies, ladybirds and other fascinating insects. We would watch with wonder as mango trees bloomed, catch the whiff as jackfruit trees sprouted buds that would in course of time transform into giant fruits, and eat the crunchy tender cucumbers that farmers would let us pluck. We believed that the single-log bridges across the streams were for the grown-ups; for us there was the gurgling stream to slosh across. Not for a moment did we worry about our clothes getting wet. After all, there was time till we reached school! And we had no fear of footwear getting wet either: we wore none!

Rainy days – about half the school year – were even more fun in the Malabar of the 1950s when "climate change" was nowhere on the horizon. Each one of us had a palm-leaf umbrella that sat firmly on the head. Since we walked in Indian file formation, we kept a safe distance, for if we went too close to the one in front or the pal behind, the two would collide, lose balance and land in the shallow waters of the paddy flats.

Our school was a thatched shed. Only the seniors had benches to sit on. The privileged class, students in Class V, had desks too. We, the juniors, in Classes I and II, sat on the floor and shared the same teacher. The working arrangement was that as those in Class I learnt what had been taught, those in Class II would be taught a new lesson. As they revised the lesson, Class I would be taught a new lesson. And so it went. Needless to add, there were some amongst us who were all ears about what was being taught to the other class!

Come monsoons, the thatched roof would permit some water to drip into the classrooms. That, too, afforded us some fun and diversion, as we could shift from our assigned spaces on the floor. When the sun shone, its rays would filter through the thatched roof and form little circles on the floor or on the books or the knickers or the frocks that the pupils wore.

The children that we were, referred to these circles as 'eggs'. It was our pastime to open our palms and stretch our hands to where an 'egg' was. We would then bring the 'egg' to the centre of the palm, close the fist and thus 'catch the egg' and pretend to put it into our pockets. Those who wore no shirts were allowed to put the eggs in their mouths. All of this, of course, only when the teacher was not around.

One day, when Leela teacher was away in Class II, my classmate Ananthan and I were busy catching eggs and putting them one by one into our shirt-pockets. At an unexpected moment, Leela teacher made her entry into the class. We were too busy to notice either her or the ambient calm that had suddenly descended. When our classmates saw her enter, they were wise enough to bury their faces in the books.

As she watched us, the entire class giggled. That was when we came down from the world we had created. Leela teacher called both of us to the table and asked us to stretch out our hands, palms open. She pulled out the slender cane. Ready to receive one lash, if not more, I shut my eyes hard, waiting for the cane to hit my palm and suffer the sting coursing through my body. So did Ananthan.

I heard the swish of the menacing cane as it cut through the air. I winced as I heard it hit the target, but it was not my palm. I heard a titter run through the classroom and wondered why. The cane had landed on, I guess, Ananthan's palm, because it never hit me. I waited for my turn.

Nothing happened. Leela teacher said, "Go back to your seats, both of you." I wondered why I had been spared and only Ananthan was punished. Heads down, not looking at each other, the two of us went back to our seats.

On our way back home, Ananthan asked me, "Did it hurt, Rajan?"

I responded, "Weren't you, Ananthan, the one that got the caning?"

The way both of us were "hit" with just one swish, the first corporal punishment I received in school, without hurting either of us is perhaps the sweetest memory I have of my Class I days and of Leela teacher.

STAR ATTRACTION

Though we were from a village, my father's frequent job transfers took us to several towns. Keen that, in the process, my brothers, sisters and I should not forget out roots and become too urbanised, Achhan kept reminding us, "Don't forget the tradition and culture we have inherited."

So, during long summer holidays, we'd be packed off to our grandparents. We too looked forward to these breaks in the village, when we could free ourselves from the tyranny of textbooks and homework – and the martinet of a father. Unadulterated merrymaking: goodies to eat, games with our cousins; cart-wheeling, cavorting and swimming in the pond by our home.

Even so, Achhan had dictated a strict regimen: morning bath, temple visit, a few pages of the basic books like the *Sidhharoopam* (The Book of Grammar), *Amarakosham* (The Book of Synonyms) and *Subhaashitaani* (The Book of Quotations) – so that we'd stay brushed up on our Sanskrit and acquire some ancient wisdom too – and a few pages of Wren & Martin's English Grammar. Selected parts of *Kerala Paanineeyam* by Raja Raja Varma on *vritta* (metre) and *alankaara* (figures of speech) were also mandatory. We had to learn these by rote and reproduce the entire matter, chapter and verse, on demand. Achhan had laid down the inviolable rule that we could go out to play only after these tasks had been completed.

Our cousins, unfettered by such shackles, would start their fun and frolic soon after breakfast. Not us. Naturally, they were objects of our envy. It was not until 11 am that we finished the chores even if we skipped a few pages and rushed through the job. And 5.30 pm was our deadline, while sunset was no bar in their case.

Turning in by 5.30, we had another bath. After prayers, we had to recite multiplication tables, mathematical formulae, the days of the week and months of the year (three versions: Malayalam, Gregorian and *Saka*) and an assortment of other things we were supposed to remember. After this, till dinner was announced, we were to be busy with a round of *aksharashlokam* (think of it as the *antakshari* of the 1950s). Achhappan, that was what we called our grandfather, was asked to ensure that we stuck to this regimen. It was painful while it lasted, but I must confess that in our later life, all this gave us a great advantage over our rivals in academics and competitive examinations.

Achhan had also asked Achhappan to take us to the village's art performances, of which there were plenty. These were mostly folk arts or temple festivals, which took place at night. A couple of times in a year, there would be *kathakali, ottan thullal* or *krishnaattam* performances in the large courtyard of our nearby ancestral house, where the Kaaranavar – head of the extended family – lived. All this legacy also had a role in keeping the wheels of the rural economy moving, Achhappan would explain: the life of local artistes was made a little more comfortable with some remuneration, grains and new clothes. Moreover, the working class had their share of free entertainment; for the women in the household, it meant a change from their chores. (And don't forget, the Kaaranavar got an ego-trip!)

Achhappan himself was well-versed in the nuances of these art forms as well as mythology. Before a performance, he would narrate to us the story to be staged. During the performance, he would 'introduce' the characters to us and patiently explain the meanings of the verses and the significance of each *mudra* (gesture).

Once, the night's kathakali performance was Duryodhana Vadham, and Achhappan had given us the story outline. The rivalry between the two sets of cousins, the tussle for the kingdom, the game of dice, Duryodhana and his brother Dusshaasana misbehaving with

Draupadi, the exile of the Pandavas, their return and their revenge over the Kauravas.

That evening, Achhan came lugging his suitcase, marking the beginning of the end of our holidays.

The performance began after dinner and would go on till daybreak. The tall bronze lamps were lit, the euphony of the musical instruments and the aroma of incense filled the air. The entire village thronged the place, their eyes shining with expectation. The traditional *thirassheela,* the curtain in black, red and green, was drawn. The performance began with Dharmaputra and Duryodhana engaged in a play of dice…

The pious Dharmaputra did not impress my eight-year-old mind as the wily Duryodhana did: his colourful make-up and gear, complete with the mace, as opposed to the plain Dharmaputra must have done the trick. As the story progressed, Dharmaputra lost the bet. Duryodhana was at his vicious best when he screamed, "I'll not give you even an inch of land." As the Pandavas proceeded for thirteen years in exile, the decibel level declined – it was life in the forest for the Pandavas and Draupadi that was featured.

I must have nodded off momentarily, but woke up with a start when I thought of my father, who would take me to task if I were caught napping. I tried to keep my eyes open, but tired as I was from the day-long frolicking with my cousins, it was hard. Achhappan understood my plight, gently stroked my back, and asked me to go to sleep.

I was more than willing to agree. I stretched myself on the reed mat, my head on his lap. Two things stood in the way. I was scared that my father would find out that I was sleeping when I should be 'getting my cultural education'. And, I was keen to see Dusshaasana in full cry.

"Please wake me up," I requested Achhappan, "when Achhan or Dusshaasana comes."

The elders seated around us broke into a loud guffaw, leaving me wondering what the joke was about.

CLOTHIER TO THE FAMILY

The other day at a shopping mall, I was dismayed by the array of clothes. What range of colours, fabrics and styles! You would just not find any identical pieces, if, for some weird reason, you wanted two.

That reminded me of my childhood. After the schools closed for the summer in March, Achhappan would start the exercise of "upgrading the family wardrobe". That, normally, was the only set of clothes bought during the year. It was also Vishu festival time; with school closed for summer, the clothes would "remain new" for a couple of more months!

It must have been a Herculean task for Achhappan to mobilise enough funds to buy cloth for the entire extended family. He perhaps had to sell of a big chunk of the coconuts harvested or use the sale proceeds of his cashew, arecanuts or whatever. Liquidity was a problem in homes that relied on agriculture – money came in only during "seasons".

The resources in place, Achhappan would set off for Tellicherry (present day Thalasseri), the big town. He would catch the "first bus" – he believed that if one had to take a bus, it had to be the first. The conductor would offer him his favourite front seat next to the driver. If that seat was occupied by some lesser mortal, the conductor would have it vacated for *Baavunnor* – the colloquial form of his title *Vaazhunnavar*, meaning "the one who administers", conferred on his forebears by the Pazhassi Raja.

Though Achhappan was not expected back until lunchtime, breakfast onwards, everyone would wait eagerly for him. All ears would perk up for the vehicle's horn and, for the next ten minutes – the time it would take for him to tread from the main road to our compound – all eyes would be riveted on the gate.

Finally, he'd emerge by about 2 pm, followed by helpers Kittan or Chanthu or Chaatthu carrying two huge bales of cloth, each containing about 30 yards (called a "kutthu", I think). It was often small checks – white and blue – or white and red; or white and black; or white and grey. There was my first lesson on the economies of scale.

Everyone in the family – male, female, young or old – would get a garment from the same fabric. In an unwitting demonstration of feudal socialism, the servants too would get clothes from the same roll!

Checks were not *de rigeuer,* though: occasionally, deviations were permitted. I have an old group photograph taken in a year when stripes was the theme: men and boys wear striped shirts, all women are in striped blouses and all the girls are in striped frocks or skirts. It's a sepia print, but my mother distinctly recalls the stripes were navy blue.

Shirts being of the same material, and more or less the same size, used to be the grounds for disputes. One brat, having stained his shirt (cashew-fruit sap being the main culprit), would stealthily replace it with that of a cousin who hadn't stained his. Indeed, in time the ownership of a shirt was often established by the nature, size and location of a stain: "That shirt with the small tender mango stain on the left pocket is Bhaskaran's!"

Trousers hadn't yet arrived in our villages: men wore white *mundu* (unstitched garment for the lower half of the body). Toddlers wore a red *konakam* (loincloth); small boys had *thorth* (loosely-woven, quick-drying, white towel used in Kerala) and the bigger among boys wore a small mundu.

Ananthan was the village tailor who made shirts, blouses, frocks and skirts for all. Alterations and repairs too were part of his services. It was his practice to visit the toddy-shop after work. The frothy white liquid would loosen his strained muscles and a relaxed Ananthan, now a happier man, would walk back home, a song on his lips.

On his return from Tellicherry with the cloth, Achhappan would send word for Ananthan to come by nightfall and take measurements. On such days, the tailor would not visit the toddy shop, not daring to appear before Baavunnor in an inebriated state.

There was always a lurking suspicion that the tailor would "swallow" some of the cloth. So, if the cloth was for, say, eight shirts, orders would be placed for nine: "After all, these are little boys!" But you couldn't outwit the tailor, who would ask for 18 yards where 16 was enough. Another standing instruction to Ananthan was to make the garments "a bit larger". The explanation: "Why, children grow fast".

One of the greatest applications of averages, I think, was in making shirts for the boys. Ananthan would be asked to make a shirt that both 12-year-old Unni and his 10-year-old cousin Dasan could wear. The obliging Ananthan would make a shirt that would suit an eleven-year-old, which would be tight for Unni and loose for Dasan! As for frocks: "Make Vanaja's a little long; she's shooting up!" That frock would tickle her ankles in the first year and her knees in the last year of its life – and fit her perfectly for a few months in between!

Finally, the tailor would promise to deliver all the garments on 13 April. "No!" the elders would scream.

That would be too late. Vishu falls on the 14th and we would not be able to wash (you didn't wear new clothes touched by others) and dry them before the festive day. "Give them at least on 10 April," all would plead. After a lot of haggling, Ananthan would agree, "Okay, on the 12th."

Ananthan's woes would start from that day. As Vishu approached, we would pass his shop one by one to detect any progress: has he at least cut the cloth? We dared not enter his workplace, or peer into his glazed wooden cupboard to find out. He might not even have opened our bundle! As 12 April drew near, we would muster some courage and start pestering him. At last, he would open the bundle and start cutting the cloth. It did not matter whose shirt – or blouse or frock – he stitched first because Achhappan had given him strict instructions against any piecemeal delivery, because that would destroy peace at home!

With all that, if it were not for Ananthan, Vishu would not have been as splendid!

DI IDLI, DA DOSA ...

At one time, Koodali High School was the only high school within a 15-kilometer radius of my home. It had humble beginnings, having been upgraded from a *kalari* (a school where children were imparted basic education) where, more than a hundred years ago, a *gurukkal* (teacher) taught the Malayalam alphabet to local children. Upon the gurukkal's death, it was taken over by a visionary Kaaranavar of the family, who set up an elementary school in its place. A couple of decades later, when my mother was still a student, it was elevated to a middle school. It became a reputed high school by the 1940s and has been alma mater to thousands of higher secondary students. Koodali High School was once adjudged the best school in Kerala. The school belonged to my own Tharawaad and was run by our Kaaranavars. The teachers, mostly men, were often my relatives. One noted exception – on both counts – was Yashoda Teacher, my First Form class teacher.

Yashoda Teacher, who also taught us English, was a very stern woman. While most of the other teachers treated the children "from the family" with kid gloves, she would have none of it. For her, all her pupils were equal. And none dared complain (against not being given preferential treatment)!

Compared to my classmates, I had a sort of disadvantage: a reputation to live up to! My mother, too, had once been her student and evidently a good one. Whenever I made a mistake, Yashoda Teacher would say, "I never expected this from Devi's son" or "Devi was a quick learner."

Yashoda Teacher was herself possibly taught by British teachers, as her clipped accent revealed. Till she taught me how to, I used to pronounce words like shirt and skirt with a marked stress on the R, as most Keralites do.

And, today, when I hear or see a question tag, I am often reminded of Yashoda Teacher. In Malayalam, tag questions end mostly with negatives – *alle? ille?* (no?) – and, so, we tend to carry that legacy into English and ask, for instance, "You haven't brought your pencil, no? She was the one who drilled it into our heads that the better form of the tag question is to end with a positive instead: "You haven't brought your pencil, have you?"

Malayalis are the butt of several jokes on the way we pronounce words like simply, loan, gold or gulf. They often become "zimbly", "lawn", "gauld" and "gelf". If I do not get railed for such transgressions, the credit should go to Yashoda Teacher. There was a time when I could, for the life of me, never tell between the two pronunciations of "the". Although I had been taught that we should use the short "da" before a consonant and the long "di" before a vowel sound, my addled young brain was confused even between consonants and vowels.

Yashoda Teacher removed the doubt once and for all by saying: "Di *idli* (a typical item of South Indian breakfast made by steam-cooking a rice-lentil batter), da *dosa* (another item resembling a pan-cake, made of rice); da three idlis, di eight dosas." I have never forgotten her idli-dosa formula.

Some of my classmates were my cousins. Traditionally, even if a cousin was older by a day, one had to respect them with the honorific suffix *ettan* for boys and *echi* or *edatthi* for girls.

One day, Yashoda Teacher asked me to read aloud a passage from the textbook. I fidgeted. My book was with Mohanettan (Rear Admiral K Mohanan in later life). I had kept a beautifully dried fern leaf between its pages and given it to him. He had agreed to give me a matchbox label featuring a tiger and a goat in exchange.I leaned towards Mohanettan seated in the next row to take my book. Yashoda Teacher's eagle eye did not miss that surreptitious move. "Rajan, where's your book?" she asked.

"With Mohanettan."

Yashoda Teacher frowned: "He may be your ettan at home. In school, he is just Mohanan, okay?"

I nodded.

Another life lesson: Never carry personal relationships into one's professional life – a credo I've lived by. It's my greatest tribute to Yashoda Teacher.

MOOSORE

The children called him Moosore, but his real name was Narayanan Nambiar. Why? Moosore is the colloquial form of the word *mootthavar* – "the senior" – in what was North Malabar in today's Kerala. Old "Naaraanan Moosore" was the cook in our branch of some fifty people from a large matriarchal joint family. Short and stocky, he was also bald but his body was so hairy, it was difficult to say where his facial hair ended and torso hair began!

Moosore was a man of regular habits. Up before five, he'd take a dip in our village pond and start his day's work. His first job – even as the several other helpers and maids of the household arrived – was to put the huge canister of coffee in the dining room for his 'clients' to help themselves to as and when they wanted. It wasn't exactly bed-coffee. The earlier one got up, the hotter Moosore's coffee would be! Having to drink it cold would be a disincentive for getting up late. A condition of eligibility for the coffee was a set of clean teeth.

The coffee canister in place, Moosore would turn to his next task – deciding on and preparing breakfast. It was usually idli because it's easy to mass produce. Moosore poured the batter in a banana-leaf-lined round colander, then steamed it in the large idli-pot. So what came out was a large, flat idli-cake, which he'd cut into two-inch cubes. I preferred the arc-shaped ones from the edges. Coconut chutney was the unchanging side-dish.

Meanwhile, the women of the house would all be bathed and ready to serve breakfast for the children who had to go to school. Most of the employed men of the family worked as teachers or other school staff. The school, run by the family, was in those days, the only employer in the village. By then Moosore would get busy preparing lunch, ordering his assistants and the other maids around. He would not relax until noon, when the tiffin carriers to be sent to the school were all ready.

That done, Moosore would go to the pond again for an elaborate bath. He would carry a piece of Sunlight bar-soap, a thorth, the loosely-woven thin quick-drying Kerala towel, and a fresh mundu. He'd dab coconut oil on his bald pate and massage his body with an Ayurvedic oil.

As a toddler too young to go to school, I would accompany him to the pond with other children. Moosore then descended the steps of the pond dressed only in a loincloth and placed his portly frame in the still waters. He would then swim across the length of the pond a few times, as we watched in awe. He would oblige us by diving into the pond, at times doing an aerial somersault.

It was a spectacular sight when he finally emerged from deep down at some faraway spot. Out of the water, the otherwise unruly fuzz on his torso, arms and legs would all be tamed and clinging to his body now. We watched as he applied soap on the mundu he'd worn and washed it. He then used the same soap on his body too. Even today when I think of Moosore, I get the smell of Dhanwantaram oil mixed with Sunlight soap! One more dip and he would wipe himself dry and head back home in his crisp white mundu.

After his lunch, he was free till about 6 pm, when dinner had to be cooked. (Evening coffee and snacks were the portfolio of our two maids, Ammaalu Amma and Chiruthai Amma.) This was when Moosore would catch his forty winks in the outhouse. Nobody dared make a noise or disturb him while he rested.

His siesta would end by the time the younger lot returned from the school. That's when he would fashion toy watches and spectacles, balls and snakes, windmills and trumpets using coconut fronds. Leaves, flowers and fruits of wild plants would transform into toys that would forever fascinate us.

Moosore was at his peak of activity when large-scale cooking (as if cooking for fifty was not large enough!) was required – for weddings and festivals. He led the pack of cooks and other hands that joined in from the other branches of the family. Managing the store-room and provisions, he would ration out supplies and oversee everything from the slicing of vegetables to the cooking. Moosore was a study in concentration when tasting samples of *sambar, olan, koottukari, naarangaakkari* or the *paayasams*.

Speaking of paayasams, Moosore would make one of the many varieties of this delicacy on certain days. He knew exactly the birthdays of every family member. "Next Monday is Chitra of Karkitakam – Girija's birthday," he would say and you can bet your shirt there would be paayasam for lunch. With 50 members, the average was a paayasam a week.

For long, I did not know that Moosore had a wife and children – he was so much a part of our household, it had never occurred to me that he too had a family.

Nearly two decades later, on a cool Sunday afternoon, I was enjoying a picnic with friends in Bedaghat near Jabalpur, MP, where I was posted on my first job. We were in a boat and our oarsman-cum-guide took the boat to the maze of waterways enveloped by marble rocks. He sang a few lines of "*O basanti pawan paagal*", adding, "We're at the scenic spot in the film *Jis Desh Mein Ganga Bahti Hai* where Vyjayanthimala breaks into this song."

You're not going believe this, but right then, the old, familiar smell of Sunlight soap and Dhanwantaram oil wafted, inexplicably, into my nostrils. I felt that it was rather queer, but left it at that.

A letter I received from my grandmother the next week had the following line: "Naaraanan Moosore passed away peacefully last Sunday during his afternoon nap."

GRANDPA'S GAMBIT

Every Friday evening, with little me in tow, Achhappan would amble towards the plantain trees. With a pen-knife, he'd snip a couple of fully-grown plantain leaves. He would then carefully cut out and segregate the spines of the leaves for me to carry home for his weekly ritual.

Achhappan would splice and carve the spines into specified shapes to fashion two sets of pieces for playing *chaturangam* (an Indian version of chess). The thick end would become the king, the slender pieces would make the pawns. The minister, the chariot, the horse and elephant (not queen, rook, knight or bishop) were made from the remaining portions.

That was part of our preparation for the weekly visit of Maadhavammaaman, headmaster of the local school, who would play chaturangam with him. He was not just Achhappan's sparring partner: the former's daughter had married the latter's son. The two would spend the weekends in each other's company pursuing their common interests – poetry, Sanskrit, classical music, aksharashlokam, literature, politics, and, of course, astrology before the game. On Monday morning, Maadhavammaaman would depart to reach his school well before the first bell. This was a routine practised for over a decade.

Maadhavammaaman was a great puzzler. I used to think that the only pastime he did not share with Achhappan was the cryptic crossword in The Hindu. He had picked up the skill while in college; being self-taught, Achhappan,could just about manage to read English. However, Achhappan, on the other hand, was a Sanskrit scholar. His magnum opus was the *vrittaanuvritta, padaanupada tarjima* – metre-to-metre, word-for-word translation – of Kalidasa's *Abhijnaana Shaakuntalam* into Malayalam. (Later, the redoubtable Sardar K M Panicker and Vallathol Narayana Menon, the titan of Malayalam literature, were impressed by this work and urged him to publish it. It came out with an introduction by Panicker and a critique with rich encomiums by Vallathol himself.)

They would exchange pleasantries sipping the hot tea, which Achhamma my grandmother, made as soon as Maadhavammaaman came in trudging down the laterite stone-paved path flanked by crotons and hibiscus. After the cuppa, there was a mandatory walk in the sylvan paddy-fields discussing a poem that had appeared in the recent issue of the Mathrubhoomi weekly or a story in Mangalodayam. This would be followed by an elaborate ritual of washing the feet, hands and face in the pond.

The two men would then walk back to their favourite spot, a wooden platform in the sit-out, and place themselves a few feet apart, each leaning against a pillar. Achhappan would use charcoal to reinforce the fading lines of the 8 x 8-inch square drawn on the wooden platform. I was like Snowy in the Tintin comics, their constant companion (without any entertainment value but not much of a nuisance either). I would look forward to Friday evenings and the rendezvous between the two.

More serious business followed. They could be seen discussing the post-Partition trauma. It could as well be a debate on some aspect of a planet in astrology. Well versed in Sanskrit, they would at times attempt a verbal translation into Malayalam of a passage from Kalidasa's *Abhijnaana Shaakuntala*.

After dinner, they would shift gears to a series of chaturangam games. Few words would be spoken after that, but you'd hear grunts and hmm…'s, which had specific meanings – a doubt, a question, an exclamation, a challenge, a compliment – depending on the variations in the pitch, length and intonation of a grunt or hmm…And the game, aided by a hurricane lamp, would go well past midnight, interrupted only for paan-chewing sessions.

That Friday evening looked no different. The usual routine ensued: pleasantries, tea, walk, some nuances of poetry and astrology. A bath in the water in the huge urn getting heated in the hearth fired by dried coconut fronds in the bathroom would be followed by dinner and then the chaturangam session would begin. As they entered the grunts-and-hmm…'s zone, I felt sleepy. My head on Achhappan's lap, I lay on the mat and dozed off.

It must have been a little – or a long – while later. Gently lifting my head off his lap, Achhappan said, "Let me fetch some water." It disturbed my slumber. Achhappan walked towards the kitchen.

From the corner of my eye, I watched Maadhavammaaman's left hand moving towards the square. In a swift, but stealthy movement, he snatched a piece – his opponent's – and flung it into the darkness of the courtyard.

When Achhappan returned, it was Maadhavammaaman's turn to take a break. Using the opportunity, I sneaked to Achhappan on Maadhavammaaman's strange and unethical action. "Shhhhh…!" Achhappan admonished me softly, "Will speak to you later. Go to sleep!" Achhappan lost that game.

Later, I asked Achhappan about Maadhavammaaman's impropriety and his own cool response to it. "The game was in a stage," Achhappan explained, "where unless he did that, he would lose." I could not digest that one. "But why should you let him win?"

"You have to let others win too," Achhappan explained, "if you want to continue playing." That did not quite sink into my six-year-old mind. He added, "At such critical stages, I always go to fetch water or some betel leaf."

ORANGES, ANYONE?

As was the custom in those days, Achhappan had moved into his bride's matriarchal household near Cannanore after he got married in the early 1930s. Though born into a family of Vedic and Sanskrit scholars, Achhappan was used to hard work, physical labour and a tough life. By contrast, the men in her family, all traditionally landed gentry, were not used to any activity that meant sweating it out; they only supervised their farm-related activities.

For the young man newly inducted into an affluent joint family, this was traumatic. He had time on his hands, a lot of it, and nothing to do. Control of farm labour was the portfolio of the men of the family, and the sons-in-law were not to be burdened with such responsibilities.

The forenoon's schedule began with an early-morning bath and a visit to the temple, followed by a hearty breakfast. After that there was precious little to be done. He had to be generally busy doing nothing all day. And married couples were allowed each other's company only after dinner.

Achhappan was not alone in this predicament. There were other such young men, too, married into the family. They would engage themselves in pastimes like exchanging jokes or gossip, card games, a siesta and such other unproductive activities.

But how long can you put an enterprising young man down, tying him to an epicurean life? Achhappan was raring to go. And he did. He bought himself a secondhand truck (a Buick, Chevrolet, Leyland, I can't recall what he said) and learnt to drive it.

Achhappan would buy coconuts from the village and sell them in Mysore, over a hundred miles east. Early on Friday mornings, he would set off on his truck, with Kittan, his Jeeves, for company. After the sale, he would buy Coorg oranges from Mysore's wholesale market the next day, bring them to coastal Cannanore and sell them. It made sound economic sense.

This went on for long. During one such trip on a bright October day, the orange-laden truck stalled and soon seized up. Misery never comes alone: a flat tyre compounded the problem.

It was nearing noon. There was no workshop nearby. Someone told Achhappan that help would be available only at Virajpet in the west or Nanjangud in the east. Virajpet, another person said, was ill-equipped and it may be better to engage the Nanjangud mechanic. With no telephones, the only way out was to go and fetch him.

So, while Achhappan stayed with the oranges Kittan hitched a ride on another truck. After six long hours, he returned alone. When he reached Nanjangud, the only mechanic in the workshop was winding up for the day. He was also leaving for his village, and the earliest he could return was on Monday if all went well. His pregnant wife was in hospital.

It was also the *Dussehra* season. In case he could not turn up on Monday, it was going to be worse: that evening, his tools would be kept away for worship, for the next day was *Aayudha Pooja* and no worker worth his salt would touch any tools till *Vijaya Dashami* on Wednesday morning.

That was bad news. Kittan and Achhappan would have to keep watch over the oranges for three, if not four, days. And exposed to the elements, the ripe and succulent oranges in the hold of the truck would by then be useless.

Other vehicles sped past. Some truck drivers would slow down or stop to enquire, say a few sympathetic words and move ahead. Achhappan toyed with the idea of persuading a driver to ferry the oranges to Cannanore for sale, but that would mean abandoning his own truck in wilderness.

Sensing that Achhappan had no choice other than a distress sale of the oranges, some enterprising truck drivers offered to buy the fruits at about ten percent of the cost. But incurring a ninety percent loss was not his idea of business.

Villagers, several of them tribals, were returning home after work with bags and baskets of rice and other provisions they'd bought from the market. Watching them, Achhappan had a bright idea and surprised passers-by. He announced that they could pick up as many oranges as they wanted and carry them home for their children!

Rather than incur a huge loss, he would be Santa Claus for at least a day. Call that making a virtue of necessity.

A RIDDLE WRAPPED IN AN ENIGMA

Nobody knew how or why Swamy came to live with us.

He was found one morning by Achhappan when he, as usual, woke up at five and opened the front door. In the blur of the setting moon, he noticed a human figure lying on the floor at the far end of the open verandah. Achhappan went back in and fetched a lantern to check on the uninvited guest. Deep in slumber was a lanky, unshaven, hungry-looking man in his mid-fifties, wearing nothing more than a thorth. Achhappan's initial reaction was to wake him up and interrogate him, but no, he decided to let him sleep.

In thirty minutes, Achhappan was back after his bath and coffee. Seated in his easy chair in the verandah, its long arms bridged with his writing plank, Achhappan lit the kerosene table lamp on the side-table. He then carefully placed his dip pen and inkpot somewhere on the right half of the plank. Soon he was engrossed in his literary pursuit.

In a while, the rays of the rising sun woke up our guest. He opened his eyes, sat up and smiled at Achhappan, who smiled back. His answers to Achhappan's queries were either vague or philosophical.

"What is your name?"

"People call me Swamy because I sport a beard and recite *stotram* (prayers) and *shlokam* (verse). They think I am a saint."

"Where do you belong?"

"One belongs to a place this moment and to another the next. Can anyone say with certainty that he belongs to a particular place?"

"Any relatives?"

"Everyone in this world is related to me."

Sending out a strong signal that he did not want any more conversation on his origins, Swamy walked towards the pond for a bath.

When he returned, he was in the same now-damp thorth. Achhappan asked Achhamma to get him a mundu, but Swamy declined. "Get me another thorth," he said. "I wear only a thorth." He then demanded a cup of tea, which he enjoyed sipping as he hummed a folk song.

Around half past seven, Achhappan went to the garden, where he had a vegetable patch with brinjals and okra, chillies, various beans, tapioca, plantains and the like. An hour each, spent every morning and evening, making the garden beds, weeding, watering and plucking any dead leaves – that was his idea of wholesome exercise. Swamy followed him around, helping and fetching water from the pond for the plants. Neither spoke a word, but they coordinated their moves well.

We were served breakfast in the *antaraalam*, or dining room, which connected the main building and the kitchen. Meanwhile, Swamy, seated cross-legged on the floor, had his breakfast served on a plantain leaf in the verandah.

After that, Swamy borrowed a knife from Kalyani, our cook, and proceeded to the "estate", where he pruned the plantain trees, tied up the pepper vines for support, and – all this was unassigned – did a lot of odd jobs till it was lunchtime.

After lunch, when the older family members withdrew to their rooms for a siesta, Swamy too slept on the veranda floor. Evening tea taken, he'd find more work to do, then take a dip in the pond. After that, Swamy went for a stroll to the village market beyond the unending stretch of paddy fields, only to return in time for supper.

Surely, Achhappan found in him a helping hand. Achhamma would at times request him to fetch some provisions during his evening walks. He never demanded any payment for his services – nor was he offered any money. Swamy marked his attendance regularly for meals, which was all he needed.

There was a problem, however. My urbane uncle, a banker in the district headquarters, took an instant dislike for Achhappan's new-found Jeeves with his dishevelled salt-and-pepper hair, unruly beard and hairy chest. Uncle was quite upset on seeing Swamy when he came home for the weekend. No, it was not just the looks of the man who wore nothing but a thorth that repelled him. "What do you know of this guy to offer him shelter here?" he asked Achhappan. "He could be a criminal on the run. He may loot you and decamp one night. How can you ever trust a man who just strays in?"

Yet Achhappan, firm in his conviction that Swamy was not up to any mischief, pacified my uncle. "He helps us a lot," Achhappan explained, "he's a good fellow. Let him stay." Uncle did not press the point further and so Swamy became part of our household.

Achhamma would hand Swamy a tenner at times and ask him to buy sugar or green gram or maybe just some salt from Moosa Hajee's shop, which he would gladly do. But Swamy would keep the coin-change and return to my grandmother only the notes that Moosa gave back. In the initial days, Achhamma would ask him, "Swamy, how about the six-and-a-quarter annas?" Avoiding eye contact, he would, depending on his mood, respond, "Oh, that? I took it," or "Looks like I dropped it somewhere" or "I made an offering at the temple."

He did that with small amounts of money, no matter who it belonged to. One evening, my uncle gave him a rupee and asked him to get a packet of Passing Show cigarettes. An hour went by, two, three ... but there was no sign of Swamy. Finally, at around nine all of us went to sleep. Next morning, when questioned, he replied, "As it was Muharram, Moosa's shop was shut." So, how about the money? Without batting an eyelid, he replied, "But Kannan's arrack shop was open."

Swamy would spend the small change he appropriated to buy himself beedis or a fish curry meal in Ambu's, the only eatery in the village, or on the occasional drink. On days he planned to eat out or have a drink, he would announce to nobody in particular, "I'll be late tonight." That meant he didn't need supper. Nobody knew when he returned after the revelry, but the next morning he would behave as if nothing had happened!

Swamy was outspoken to a fault. In retrospect, I suspect he took advantage of the impression that others had about his being an oddball and an eccentric. Our kitchen was strictly vegetarian, which Swamy was not too happy about. "The reason why all of you have to wear spectacles from an early age," he would say, "is that all you eat is grass and leaves. Eat some fish and meat and see the difference!"

On that point, Swamy and my uncle agreed. Though initially not well-disposed towards him, uncle had a pact with Swamy: on Saturdays, Swamy would bring some fish from the market, which he would cook in a makeshift hearth in a far corner of the large compound. The two of them would polish off the entire stuff and look forward to the next weekend.

Swamy refused to wear anything more than his thorth. He had no use for mats or pillows or sheets: rain or shine, in sickness or in health, he would sleep only on the verandah floor, exactly where Achhappan had first found him.

But he was also a man of moods. On certain days, he would be quiet, and not speak even if spoken to. On others, he would go about singing aloud, unmindful of who was around. And although he could not read or write, his repertoire was quite large – ballads, nonsense verse, prayers, astrology, *keertans, kathakalipadams, ottan thullal* verses, classic poetry, slogans from the freedom movement – his memory was phenomenal. When my sisters taught him rhymes like Twinkle, Twinkle, Little Star or Hickory, Dickory Dock and *Saare jahaan se acchha Hindustaan hamaara,* his range went to another level.

We would never know more about Swamy – his background, his family, his relatives. Enquiries by different people on different occasions during his twelve-year stay with us elicited no information except that he wanted to be called Swamy.

One morning, as usual, when Achhappan opened our front door at five, he noticed that there was nobody at the far end of the open verandah. "One belongs to a place this moment and to another the next," Swamy had said. And that was it.

Nobody knows why Swamy left us or where he went. A true avadhoot Swamy was.

LATIF, ZAMBEZI AND PARENTING

A novice treading warily into the e-world, I was introduced to the 'net' by my then school-going son Gautam. I could barely navigate my way to a website, while he astounded me with his prowess at the PC. As his fingers danced about the keyboard with a dozen windows open, he'd listen to music, read the news, look up references for his homework, read up on the genome project which fascinated him and prepare for next weekend's quiz.

One day my older son Hari told us, "Anil Grover has switched from civil engineering at IIT Kharagpur to an integrated MSc course in mathematics." We wondered how he knew because after we left Patiala in 1996 following my transfer, there was practically no contact between Hari and his classmate except for a letter or two. Their correspondence had petered out; perhaps because Anil's father had also been transferred and they had left without a forwarding address.

"How did you come to know this?" asked my wife.

"Through batchmates.com," Hari beamed.

Next Sunday I sat before the computer, my wife peering over my shoulders at the screen, to see if I could use that website to find any long-lost friend. With some help from Gautam, I thought I'd start with my schooldays and then progress to university. It was rather easy, I could go to Koodali High School in Kerala's Kannur district. Soon the class of 1961 popped up on the screen. Yes, there was Latif, my bosom pal. Though we had shared a class bench for just one year, we had maintained contact for a decade after that, but the thread had snapped sometime around his marriage.

I looked up the details: he was in England now. The father of two girls, he was running The Zambezi, an inn in Middlesex. He was manufacturing and selling personalised stationery under the brand name Zambezi. He also ran The Zambezi Store. "But, of all things, why Zambezi?" Hari asked. "That's a river in Africa!"

Zambezi did ring a bell, but just then I couldn't quite recall what it signified. That night, as I lay awake waiting for my eyes to droop and 'sleep, perchance to dream', I tried to clear the cobwebs of my mind ... and, suddenly, it came back.

A popular boy in our village, Latif was the man for all jobs. Not one who had set much store by the virtues of academic achievement, he was there to pedal his way to town on a hired bicycle to fetch a doctor to attend to an immobilised patient; to assist in the erection of a pandal for the annual Uroos in the mosque, or to distribute bit notices announcing the arrival in town of Gemini Circus or an MGR-starrer like Naan Aanayittaal.

One afternoon, in biology class, it was just after the two-day Theyyam festival ended in the village. Latif had spent an active night in the fairground assisting his father, who was selling balloons and bangles, plastic whistles and palmyra sirens, rubber balls and catapults. Naturally, he nodded off in class while Vasudevan Master was holding forth on the digestive system. His eagle eyes caught Latif napping.

Stopping briefly, he asked, "Which gland produces bile, Latif? Stand up and answer!"

Rudely woken up from his siesta, Latif stood up and looked around for a helpful hint.

Ravi, known for his practical jokes, who was sitting right behind Latif poked him lightly with a pencil and whispered, "Zambezi."

"Zambezi," echoed Latif with an air of confidence.

And so, the moniker 'Zambezi Latif' stuck.

Latif hadn't abandoned his roots despite traversing continents, I was convinced, as I peered at batchmates.com.

That day, an older Latif story also came to mind.

When I was promoted to Class Ten, Latif was already there, repeating the year. He once confided in me that having failed in several classes, he'd forgotten the exact number of years he spent at school! And, years later, I'd once told his grandmother that I was Latif's classmate. "That's what half the village says," she replied.

To say that as a child, Latif was mischievous would be a huge understatement. He would pluck coconuts from Ramunni Nair's land and unleash goats tethered by Beepathumma. While returning from school, Latif's mundu would sometimes double as a net to catch fish from the temple pond. Mango seasons saw complaints about him peak: his missiles aimed at the tempting fruits would land on roofs, breaking a tile or two.

It was the last day of the half-yearly examinations. As soon as I finished, I turned in my paper and went to the loo. Soon Latif too walked in, lit a match and burst a cracker. Scared, I ran out, only to find myself in front of Mr Charles, the drillmaster. My protestations that I knew nothing of it were not heard. When Latif emerged, he too was caught.

Both of us were brought before the headmaster, who was rather new to the village. An attempt by one of the other teachers to rescue me with a good word to the headmaster didn't help. If I was not an accomplice, why was I at the scene of the crime? Yet, being a first-time offender, I was lucky to be let off with a severe reprimand and three cracks on each palm.

Latif was caned too but was told he would be suspended unless his father came in person and met the headmaster, when school reopened after Christmas.

Obviously, Latif could not tell his father that he had been summoned for such a transgression. What could he do?

When school reopened, Latif arrived accompanied by a man in a vest and *lungi* (a coloured mundu, often chequered or with bold prints) held in place with an *arappatta* (a broad and colourful belt with a couple of pockets). One could not miss his large round bloodshot eyes and muscular body. He was the local butcher, coaxed by Latif to act as his father – for a whole rupee as his fee.

'Father' and the son were ushered before the headmaster, who reeled out a list of charges. The headmaster also talked of the time Latif put Kuttan's cat in a milk powder can and used it as a football; when Latif poured water in the watchman's lantern, besides several other pranks.

The 'father' was furious. He turned to Latif, grabbed his right ear and boxed it hard. "Scoundrel! Dare you do such things again!" he shrieked, taking his role a bit too seriously. The butcher also slapped Latif hard a couple of times. Had the headmaster not intervened, more whacks would have followed.

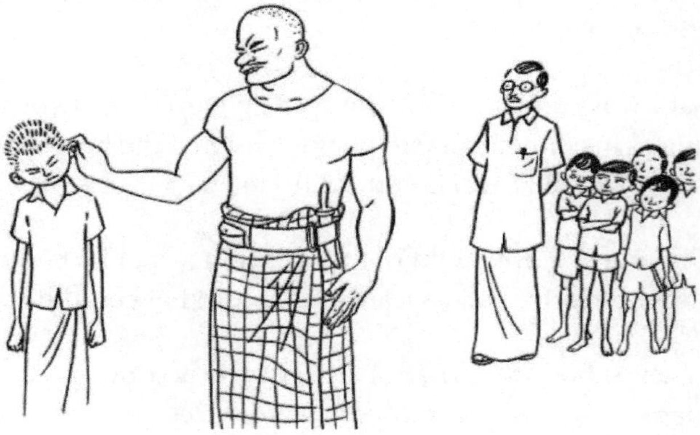

While returning home that day, Latif told me he should just have brought his real father. "The penalty would have been far less severe, and I'd have not wasted a rupee!"

Pa-renting had failed!

CANTEEN MA'SH

This morning it was *"puttum kadalayum"* for breakfast. (In Malabar, it is pronounced "pittum kadalyoom" but what's in a name?)

Fancy menu cards of restaurants with names like Banana Leaf or Coconut Grove may describe the combo dish as "Coarsely powdered rice steamed in a special mould with liberal doses of grated coconut … served with black chickpeas cooked in coconut milk and garnished with coriander, spices and curry leaves". The description might sound verbose and florid, but in fact, what's described in the first part is bland compared to the "served with" side dish – *kadala,* the chickpeas curry, which is simply divine.

Bhawani served me a portion of the piping hot hemisphere of puttu and some kadala curry. She waited for my response as I picked up a tiny pea and put it into my mouth. I said nothing.

"How is it?" she asked.

"Nice."

"Does that mean it is not as good ___?"

For either of us, the blank did not need to be filled; it meant "as that of Canteen Ma'sh". And thereby hangs a tale from the mid-1950s.

I was in the First Form of Koodali High School. Students who lived nearby would trot home for lunch. The more affluent households would send servants over with tiffin carriers. Those who stayed far away would bring packed lunches. In case lunch was not ready before a student started for school, parents would give them small change to buy whatever was available at the school canteen, run by Kunhiraman Nambiar. Kids like me envied those who did not live close by, because they could have the goodies in the canteen. In our case, rain or shine, Kunhambu would bring lunch for my cousins and me. So we were denied any opportunity to visit the canteen.

Always dressed in an ochre-coloured short-sleeved *khadi* (coarse, handloom material made of hand-spun yarn) shirt and white khadi mundu with a broad green border, he would sit at the canteen's cash desk.

Students referred to Nambiar as "Canteen Ma'sh" (short for "master", in Malayalam). There was, likewise, a "Clerk Ma'sh" in the school's office and a "Store Ma'sh" in the school's stationery and bookshop.

The closest I came to the canteen was as we marched single file to the playground for Charles Ma'sh's PT classes ("chaaRR-less" was how we pronounced his name). My mouth would water at the aromas. In those days, one hardly ever ate out, and so anything from the canteen was a dream!

Then, one day, my dream came true. There was some glitch at home. Maybe my aunt who ran the kitchen had to travel, maybe Kunhambu was laid up, I can't remember. Whatever, my uncle gave each of us a quarter anna – the round copper coin with a hole in the centre, if you remember – and told us to "have something from the canteen for lunch."

I put the coin in my shirt pocket. Every few minutes, I would feel the pocket to check if it was still there. Once, when I bent down to pick up something, it fell out and rolled. Running after it and grabbing it, I put the coin in the pocket of my shorts – safer, I reckoned.

Nothing that Yashoda teacher or Jayakesari teacher said that morning entered my head, which was speculating on what would be available in the canteen and what my quarter would fetch. Occasionally, I would put my hand into the pocket to caress the coin.

Finally, after the 1 pm bell, I ran to the canteen and placed the coin on Canteen Ma'sh's desk. "What do you want?" he asked.

Just then I realised that, having not been there earlier, I had no idea what was on offer. Thinking quickly, I did the smart thing: I pointed to a boy eating at a nearby table and said, "I'll have that."

Canteen Ma'sh put the coin in the desk drawer and asked the only bearer there to give me a plate of kadala curry – nay, the most delicious plate of kadala curry of my life – served in a shallow white enamel bowl with a navy-blue rim – no spoon!

MEGHAROOPAN'S BLESSING

Poets aren't a favourite theme for movie makers. *Ivan Megharoopan* (The Amorphous man), a 2012 Malayalam biopic with Prakash Bare in the lead role is based on *Kaviyude Kaalpaadukal* (Footprints of a Poet), the autobiography of P Kunhiraman Nair (1905-78), the celebrated poet known to Keralites as Mahakavi P.

I had met him in the mid-1950s, when his poems were carried regularly in Mathrubhoomi Weekly under the pen-name 'P'. He taught Malayalam in Koodali High School, which I attended, and was known as Kavi-Ma'sh there. Those days he was not called Mahakavi; he was Bhaktakavi. He taught the seniors and not me, since I was only in the First Form.

Kavi Ma'sh was always seen in a loose, free-flowing khadi *kurta* (a man's loose garment) and white khadi mundu. The stocky bespectacled frame would amble along the winding corridor of the school, munching something all the time. He would often put his hands into his pocket and fish out groundnuts, orange or lemon-flavoured sweets or *kalkantam* – sugar candy – and offer it to students.

I was fortunate to get close to him because he was Achhappan's good friend. The two had shared a passion for poetry.

Kavi Ma'sh lived in a small room above the provision store next to the bus-stop near the school. The room could just about accommodate a single cot and a desk and chair. I recall my first visit to the place with Achhappan on a Friday evening. The wooden staircase was steep and narrow. The steps were so far apart that I, hardly nine years old then, could not use them. Achhappan carried me up, clutching at the thick rope hanging from the roof. It functioned as the banister, its knots providing grip.

Kavi Ma'sh's dingy, dusty room had surely not been swept for ages. There was no cupboard or storage. An olive-green steel trunk with rusty corners lay under the cot. A rope strung between a nail on one wall and another on the window-frame served as his wardrobe. Three soiled khadi *jubbas* (kurta) – one grey, one brick-coloured, one white – and a couple of black-bordered white khadi mundus had been tossed carelessly on to it. There were a few books and some papers on the desk.

Beedi stubs, scraps of paper and groundnut peels and shells were strewn all over the floor. The cot had no mattress, but an old green-and-white sheet was spread over it. There was more paper and books on the cot.

On entering the room, the poet welcomed Achhappan and offered him the chair. "Sit somewhere, son," he told me.

The two discussed poetry and literary matters, neither of which interested me then and so I soon went to sleep. It must have been past 7 pm when I was woken up and carried down to the bus stop. Kavi Ma'sh, standing in the verandah with no railings, bade goodbye and Achhappan responded.

The last bus from Kannur towards our village had left and the only option was to walk the distance. As it was a full moon night, the untarred road was well-lit.

Taking my schoolbag from me, Achhappan urged me to walk. We must have gone about ten steps when Kavi Ma'sh called out, "*Vaazhunnore*!" That's what people called my Achhappan.

He then came down hurriedly and said, "Do not go alone. I will come with you – and be your guest tonight." Without waiting for an answer, he kept pace with us. More discussion on literature, recital of poems and critical appraisal followed.

Kavi Ma'sh stayed with us the whole weekend. He had his bath in the pond and his meals with us. He had come with no change of clothes. Achhappan's offered him a fresh mundu taken from his trunk. Kavi Ma'sh washed his mundu in the pond while taking a bath,dried it in the sun and wore it when he left on Monday morning.

That was Kavi Ma'sh for you. He belonged to the world and the world belonged to him. Home was where he was for the time being. He had at least two wives – one in his native Bellikoth, near Kasaragod, one in Pattambi where he studied and worked for a while – and, I guess, more lovers elsewhere.

One day, Kavi Ma'sh suddenly went missing from our school. It is said that he quit in a huff following some differences with my granduncle, who owned the school. He never came back. It was learnt later that he had surfaced in Kollengode, in Palakkad district.

Like a nebulous cloud, he remained a drifter – the reason why the biopic is titled "Ivan Megharoopan" (*ivan* means "he" in Malayalam; *megharoopan* is "in the form of a cloud"). In his works – which include short stories, articles and a few plays – our Mahakavi-Ma'sh romanticized Kerala's natural beauty, juxtaposing it with the hard realities of his life and times. The autobiography, written in beautiful, lyrical Malayalam, is much-celebrated. Poetry formed the main body of his work, but nobody knows exactly how many he had penned in his five productive decades, since many of his poems are lost.

Besides enjoying his work in later years and the memories, I can aver that I own one of his "lost" poems. It's in a book he gifted to me on my 10th birthday. On the flyleaf, he had scribbled a quatrain in Malayalam. A prayer, a blessing: "May the omnipotent Lord endow you, Rajan, with energy, long life, education, prosperity and enlightenment."

IN HIS GOOD BOOKS

He was "Raamettan" (big brother Raaman) to everyone. Why, even those who were fifty years older than him called him Raamettan, though the suffix *ettan* implies seniority in age.

My memories of Raamettan were triggered recently when I chanced upon an old book of mine which had seen better days. I had picked it up from the secondhand books market in Lakdi-ka-Pul in Hyderabad in the early 1970s and "restored" it by giving it a cover to protect it from further damage – just as Raamettan used to do, with kraft paper, needle and twine, gum and scissors.

A distant relative, Raamettan was the school librarian. He had an ever-pleasant demeanour, was dark and stocky and had a nice set of white teeth. His must have been one of several nepotistic appointments there, as the school was owned by our family and even the headmaster was an uncle of mine. The fact that he was also the first cousin of the headmaster's wife must certainly have helped. Raamettan was most likely not even a matriculate. Had he been one, he would at least have been accommodated in the school's Lower Primary teaching faculty. Instead, he was parked in the library for which, in those days, one needed no special qualifications.

We had a Library Period every Friday afternoon, a welcome change from the regimen of the classroom. The library, though, was no more than a reading room for junior students like me. Only the seniors were allowed to borrow books. We went in single file to the library, where Raamettan would give us each a book of HIS choice. We would then go to a desk and read. Five minutes before the Library Period ended, Raamettan – who sat there, often mending books with kraft paper, needle and twine, gum and scissors, in between minding us – would announce that the time was up, and we would place the books on his desk.

School timings were from 10 to 4, but the library was open from 9 to 5. So, I would make abundant use of the library not just during the hours before and after classes but even during the lunch break. I would finish lunch quickly and run to the library, where I could, during these extra hours, choose my favourite books.

One such morning I was reading Volume 4 of Kottaaratthil Shankunni's *Aithihyamaala* (a book of fantasy stories). It narrated fantastic stories. In one, blood gushed out when the scythe of a tribal woman cutting grass touched the exposed tip of a rock buried in soil. In another, a thief who stole a temple offertory one night had a hallucination – that he was amidst a milling crowd at the temple festival and could not move, till the priest who arrived at dawn for the *pooja* caught him. These stories, though incredible now, stoked my pre-teen mind no end. It would not have been possible for me to read all the seven volumes in one academic year without Raamettan's help.

At times I found it distressing that a book I had started reading in the morning would often disappear in the lunch recess because some senior had borrowed it. Raamettan must have noticed my disappointment. One morning, as I was about to return a partly-read book to the shelf it belonged to, he asked me to give it to him instead. After lunch, when I was back, he took the book from his desk-drawer and gave it back to me. I read it and returned it to him, only to repeat this in the evening. That went on till I finished the book.

Raamettan spotted my passion for reading but – rules being rules – he was unable to let me borrow any books. Since I stayed with an uncle (also a teacher in the school) who accommodated six other students – four girls and two boys – like me, our kindly librarian's will to help me found a way. A couple of them were in senior classes, but not interested in reading. So Raamettan suggested they borrow the books I wanted – a perfect working arrangement.

How a little patronage in childhood helps! I owe my everlasting romance with books, my love for their very aroma, to the enchanting world Raamettan had led me to.

TRIAL BY FIRE

One character from my childhood still vivid in my mind is Bentha Kittan.

Those were the days when, apparently, there was a severe shortage of names. While the names of women in Kerala had to be from among Ammu, Ammaalu, Paaru, Devaki, Maatu or Chirutha, men answered to names like Kelan, Koman, Raaman, Krishnan, Ambu, Kammaaran or Appa.

To distinguish one Ambu from another, it was necessary to prefix the name with adjectives – like *Valiya* (the older) or *Cheriya* (the younger), which were not uncomplimentary. Some of those Malayalam epithets would not pass the test of political correctness if used these days. They were downright insulting because they referred to physical features. *Pallan* (the one with protruding teeth), *Vikkan* (stammerer), *Kullan* (dwarf), *Konkannan* (cross-eyed), *Pottan* (mute) or *Chevidan* (deaf).

Obviously, the second part of our hero's name is a corrupt form of Krishnan. If you think *Bentha* stands for the name of a house or a village (like Badiadka or Bellikoth), you're wrong. Bentha was another adjective! In northern Malabar, the letter v appearing at the beginning of a word is often pronounced b as in *bellam* (for *vellam* – water) or *baliya* (for *valiya* – big). Thus, the crude *Bentha* stands for the refined Malayalam word *ventha* which means cooked, burnt or scalded.

Bentha Kittan was a dark, scrawny man who never wore a shirt. He was mostly seen in a thin piece of cloth that barely reached his knees. He was always busy, but I have never seen him do any work. If a small crowd formed in the village for whatever reason – marriage, betrothal, death, public meeting, whatever – he would be there. Doing nothing in particular, but just acting busy.

When walking – scurrying, really – from one place to another, his eyes would be riveted to the treetops – particularly coconut and areca nut palms. This would alert the owners of the trees, for, it was common knowledge that if Bentha Kittan had set his eyes upon a tree laden with yield, the produce would be gone the next morning. No prizes for guessing how it vanished.

So, how did Kittan become Bentha Kittan?

Thereby hangs a fiery tale.

The village then had not heard of toothpastes and toothbrushes. People used mango leaves and twigs of medicinal plants for cleaning their teeth. Another common item that served the purpose was *umikkari* (burnt paddy husk). This mild abrasive was a popular cleaning agent.

The process of making umikkari was an elaborate and time-consuming one. Paddy husk would be heaped in the evening and ignited after sunset. It was a deft, delicate operation: the husk should not catch fire but gently smoulder. As the outer layer of the cone-shaped pile of husk burned, there would be a light glow. By the time this got charred and black, the household would have gone to sleep. Then the inner parts would burn, but there would be no outward glow; no sign of the burning within.

One night, Kittan was on the prowl, stealing areca nut from a tree he had set his eyes on. On his way home with the booty, he stepped on the half-burnt heap of husk. His right leg went deep into the pile. To imagine the shock, pain and trauma he underwent, remember that goldsmiths used to melt the yellow metal in the heat generated by burning paddy husk. To add to Kittan's woes, the embers got stuck to his burned flesh.

Leaving the loot behind, Kittan ran to safety, yelling loudly and waking people up.

He was christened Bentha Kittan that night.

LEAD, KINDLY LIGHT

Nanu Nair and Chacko were bosom pals. About the same age, they lived close by in our village in Malabar. While Nanu was a native there, Chacko's parents had migrated from faraway Travancore in the early 1920s. They had bought a parcel of land close to the homestead of Nanu Nair's parents. The migrants were hardworking. They cleared the wild growth and cultivated tapioca, banana and coconut. They were thrifty and invested the surplus in more land and planted rubber. In a couple of decades, the two families were on a par with each other in their economic (and hence) social status.

The two friends had studied in the same school. After high school, Nanu inherited the Village *Adhikari*'s job from his father. Chacko worked for a few years on his father's farm. When the Second World War broke out, the army launched a massive recruitment campaign. Chacko enlisted, taking a break from agriculture and his wife Mariamma. This stint took him to several places within India and abroad, introducing him to new climes, cultures and experiences.

Chacko had to return to the village when his father died, because there was nobody else to attend to the farm. So, after two decades of army service, he was granted superannuation. Nanu was delighted that Chacko was returning to the village for good. They could spend the evenings in each other's company once again.

Soon, a pattern emerged. During the day, they would be busy in their own farms. By evening, the two would, after a wash, amble towards the village market. After a while, they would walk back and end up in either of their homes, where they would chat and be in each other's company till dinner time.

Chacko would narrate his exploits in Burma or the warfront in Mongolia and Nanu would be all ears, as if hearing it for the first time. Nanu would recite romantic poems by popular Malayalam poets like Changampuzha or the naughty couplets of Venmony. Wives Mariamma or Devaki Amma, depending on which house the pals happened to be, would be at a respectable distance, often eavesdropping and enjoying their boy-talk.

The two pals were similarly placed. Both had retired from their jobs, were reasonably well off, and respected in society. Both had their pensions to supplement the income from their farms. Their children, now with families of their own, held government jobs in the nearby town. They would visit the parents during school vacations. But for those occasional reunions, it was just the old man and his wife in both the houses.

There was one difference though. And it was a major difference. Apart from the pension, Chacko had access to the military canteen, where he could pick up stuff at prices much lower than the market rates. Thus, Chacko would also cater to some needs of his friend's household too, much to the gratitude of Nanu's wife Devaki Amma.

As a retired soldier, every month Chacko was also entitled to a couple of bottles of liquor.

Come the first of every month, Nanu Nair and Chacko would catch the bus to town, go to the treasury to collect their pensions, head to the canteen for provisions and return by noon. That included the liquor.

On such days, Nanu Nair would reach his friend's house, where they would have a drink on Chacko's sit-out bench, under a hurricane lamp. It was the 1960s and electricity had not yet arrived in the village. Nanu Nair would listen, for the nth time, to Chacko's narration of his warfront exploits in Burma or Mongolia.

Then, on a monsoon day, it had rained hard throughout the morning. The pensioners could leave for the treasury only by half past eleven. By the time they returned after their routine in the town, it was three in the afternoon and still drizzling. By late evening, there was a let-up in the rain.

Chacko was waiting as Nanu Nair walked in, his feet damp from the wet grass. Chacko went in and re-emerged with the bottle of firewater. As if on cue, Mariamma appeared with two glasses and a jug of water. The usual recital of poems, recounting of stories and some jokes followed.

Though it was getting late, there was no sign of the friends winding up. Mariamma, who was feeling sleepy after the day's chores, went to bed after telling Chacko that his dinner had been laid. The two sozzled friends even traded some smutty jokes and it was half past ten by the time they decided to call it a day.

Though it was not raining, the sky was overcast. The night was dark and there were no street lights. Chacko offered his flashlight to Nanu Nair.

"No need. I know my way about here," replied Nanu, declining the thoughtful offer.

"There may be snakes and scorpions on the way," cautioned Chacko. "Carry this lantern. You can return it tomorrow."

Nanu Nair extended his right hand to receive what Chacko offered.

As Nanu Nair's footsteps receded, Chacko called out "Is the light enough? Can you see the ground you are walking on?"

"Oh, yes. Very well."

"Still, be careful! Better safe than sorry."

"Fine. Thanks!"

The next morning, what Devaki Amma saw in her sit-out surprised her as she wondered, What's Mariamma's pet parrot in its cage doing in this house?

ME, THE CINEASTE!

Even today, I cannot often stay awake through a whole movie – a throwback perhaps to my dozing off during my first movie experience! That was in Cannanore in 1953, when I was only six.

Every first Thursday of the month, the sound of drums would herald the arrival of a bullock cart in our village. Stuck to the outside of its bamboo canopy would be posters of next week's new movie in our neighbouring town's only cinema hall, 15 kilometers away. The drummer and the cart driver would distribute printed 'cinema-notices' advertising the movie. These leaflets, printed on cheap rough paper, came in different colours – yellow, green, orange, "rose" or blue.

Village kids would chase the cart, begging for a notice, which would have pictures of the film's hero and heroine, sometimes even the villain. On the back the notice, you could read the story synopsis, given, for some reason, entirely in present tense. There was a catch, though. At a critical point (like, "After many years, Asha runs into Kumar at a railway station ...") the storyline would snap, with the phrase "... the rest on the silver screen".

As I had been prohibited by family elders from running after the bullock cart ("like those urchins"), I couldn't obtain a cinema-notice, though some schoolmates let me look at the pictures and read the story bits. The first cinema-notice that came into my possession was that of the 1950 Malayalam film Laila-Majnu. To acquire that coveted green notice, I had exchanged a valued collector's item of mine: the gold-and-silver brand foil sticker with the picture of Mahalakshmi, from my Achhappan's new mundu. I folded my new acquisition and kept in my civics textbook.

I was in a flap after that. It had the hero and heroine locked in an embrace. In our home of the 1950s, this may have been outright titillating – the equivalent of a Playboy pin-up. I feared getting caught with it yet did not have the heart to throw it away.

An uncle, a First World War veteran, was the first to have seen any kind of movie in our circle – using a bioscope, at a German town. It had two parts, no sound, was so basic and only lasted five minutes! One, he said, showed a horse carriage on a lonely road leading to a mansion. The other was of two men in animated conversation. This uncle used to talk of how soldiers from different countries were entranced by those moving images.

It was another younger uncle who took me to my first movie. I was so overwhelmed that day. After an early lunch, we got to town by bus – a rickety contraption that ran on coal. Its seats were coir mattresses with wooden backrests. Its driver, a regally seated ex-serviceman with a handle-bar moustache, seemed to regard the rest of the world with absolute disdain. The conductor sat at the entrance and issued tickets. The cleaner, who himself could do with some cleaning – his clothes, face and limbs covered in soot – stood stoking the coal. I, for a two-anna half ticket, had to sit on my uncle's lap in the crowded bus as it coursed its way through the narrow tree-shrouded mud road.

Walking from the bus stand to the cinema-hall, we heard loudspeakers belt out the devotional *Ayyane Anbarkku Meiyyane ...* sung by K B Sundarambal in Avvaiyar. Uncle explained that this was the first song played every day. That was followed by a romantic song and then a comic-sounding one.

By then, we had bought tickets (five annas for my uncle and half of that for me) and taken a bench. Seated on the sand-strewn floor in front of us were those who had two-anna tickets, booing, shouting and clapping – I'd say, an equivalent of the "pit" in a Shakespearean theatre. The "silver screen" promised by the cinema-notices stood there, tantalisingly, before me.

Suddenly, the loud song stopped and so did the booing and the clapping. The lights went out, plunging the hall into a dark silence. When nothing happened for a while, the booing resumed only to die down as some white stars, plus signs, random numbers and punctuation marks – like those used to substitute swear-words in today's comics – flickered on the screen.

Soon, horses and soldiers, camels and deserts, kings, queens, rain, lightning, wind and dust ... the scenes changed quickly. I could not make a thing out of the Tamil dialogue but enjoyed the song sequences and sword-fights. Those on the floor too clapped and whistled when such scenes appeared.

About every 15 minutes or so there were interruptions – darkness and momentary silence broken by more catcalls and clapping. The projector operator had to change film reels.

At one point, the lights came on again and music blared. I thought it was all over and got up. "It's only the interval," my uncle told me "there's more." Some people went out for a smoke, though there was no need for that – many men had been smoking even while the movie was on. My uncle suggested we stay put, else others may take our seats.

During the interval, my uncle bought peanuts and orange and lemon drops for a quarter-anna each, from a vendor in the hall. He also spent half anna on a songbook containing, apart from the lyrics of the film's songs, the names of the actors, the director, script-writer, lyricists and others.

After the interval, by the second reel-change, I dozed off. As for my uncle, I recall his annoyed expression the next morning when he discovered that the songbook too was in Tamil, which none of us could read! As for me sleeping during movies, old habits die hard.

MORE LOYAL THAN THE KING

In pre-Independence days, British Malabar was part of Madras Presidency. A Legislative Council was formed by the government to represent different segments of its subjects. My uncle, Kunhikammaaran Nambiar, was elected an MLC by the landed gentry to protect their interests. It was the early 1940s, and he was still in his late thirties.

Uncle's K's life had had an interesting twist. He was in the second year at Madras Medical College when his uncle, who managed the affairs of the affluent matriarchal family, died of snakebite. This put an abrupt end to his medical education because there was no other male member to control the family's vast estate and huge assets. He was just 21 when he ascended to the position of Kaaranavar.

Having been exposed to urban life unlike his predecessors, who had lived all along in villages, K thought differently. He joined the Indian National Congress and involved himself in the Independence movement. He constructed a small building close to the market to house a reading room and library. A dispensary was opened with a compounder in attendance, who could handle minor indispositions; a doctor would come by twice a week.

He took pains to upgrade the primary school set up by his ancestors to upper primary and then to high school. All this was achieved through efficient management of the estates and other assets of the family and by deploying any surplus cash wisely. He toned up the collection of rent arrears and other incomes, which could help meet these expenses.

K was benevolent and caring. He would walk distances rather than be carried in palanquins. He had to walk to the nearest railway station in Cannanore to catch the trains to places like Kozhikode, Payyannur and Palghat to meet leaders like K P Kesava Menon, K Madhavanar or Kunhikanna Poduval and to attend public meetings. The number of such trips increased when he became an MLC.

Finding the long walk of some twelve miles, whether rain or shine, taxing, he bought a car. In those days, his was one of the few dozen cars in the whole of North Malabar.

The bus company that plied the only bus on the Cannanore-Mysore route lost its driver Narayanan when K, offering handsome incentives, poached him.

Seated in his private car, K would often offer lifts to passers-by. Only, they were not allowed inside the car, but stood on the wide-enough footboard of the 1942 Chevy.

Once – it was July – and the monsoon had unleashed its fury and for two days, there had been no let-up in the rain. The car was on its way back from Cannanore after picking up K, who had arrived by train from Madras after a Legislative Council session.

Just then, they saw a man walking on the rain-soaked country road. A basket covered with banana leaves to protect its contents rested on his head. Soon they identified him as Kumaran. A neighbor, he would often buy the farm produce from K's fields and pepper from the gardens and the yield from the coconut groves and cashew estates. Soaked to the skin, he was obviously getting back from town after selling his merchandise.

Chauffeur Narayanan, aware of his boss's habit of offering lifts to pedestrians spoke., "Shall we ask Kumaran ...?"

"Ah ... Kumaran? He hasn't kept his promise of clearing his dues before the monsoon," observed K.

"In that case, shall I splash some mud on him?" was Narayanan's instant response. Loyalty to the master and presence of mind were obviously his charms.

THE TRAGEDY OF MY LIFE

I nurtured different ambitions at different stages of my life. My earliest desire, as far as I can remember, was to become an oracle in our small village temple. Entranced, I would watch the oracle there preparing for his performance. Wearing nothing more than a short thin red towel, he would collect hibiscus and other flowers and place them on a fresh plantain leaf along with other items including turmeric powder. Armed with a blunt sword that jangled, he would start by dancing, ever so slowly to begin with. As he got into the act, the pace would quicken until it entered the frenetic zone – and in direct conversation with God. That's when it would happen – he'd hit his skull with the sword! This masochistic game would go on until those watching the spectacle were satisfied that he had lost a sufficient quantity of blood. Turmeric powder would be applied, and the oracle's forehead would be all red and yellow. To my tender mind, being hurt was a small price to pay if I could communicate directly with God!

It was in the year I started school that the dirt track connecting Cannanore and Bangalore, which passed through our village, was being upgraded. Workers were busy levelling the road, spreading gravel evenly and then pouring the steaming black liquid tar on the track under the hot summer sun. I watched all this. After about three days, a contraption I had never seen in my life appeared on the scene. Referred to as the "injun", the road-roller was coal-fired, with its two broad heavy metal wheels and a hooded cabin in which sat the driver, his hands clasping the steering-wheel.

While everyone sweated it out in the sun, there was shade wherever that 'chariot' took him. While all others toiled standing, walking or running, he worked from his seat. He was also the first to be served at tea-time. And he was so powerful that his fingers alone could move the behemoth he sat in. Wasn't I impressed? So, I wanted to be an injun-driver when I grew up.

It was during a bus journey that I discovered my next passion. There was this man whose whistle stopped and started the bus. He collected all the money. He had the authority to decide whether (and how much) to charge for luggage. He was the last word in deciding whether young ones would travel free, on a half-ticket, or full fare. As standing passengers struggled not to fall into the laps of seated ones when the bus careened and swerved, this man alone remained rock-steady. I was naturally spell-bound. A bus conductor was what I wanted to be.

The comparable job of the ticket examiner in the train, somehow, did not appeal to me. True, he was immaculately turned out in spotless white trousers, black jacket, tie and gold-braided cap, but he did not exude the authority of the bus conductor.

All these ambitions changed as I got into my teens. I first wanted to be an English professor, like Prof Madhukar

Rao of Maharaja's College in Ernakulam, who treated students as his equals and whose freewheeling classes were great fun for me. What if, some boys used to say, the secret of his pink cheeks was a dash of rouge from his wife's dressing table? He looked good and he was good. That, too, mattered to me.

And then I wanted to be a maths wizard like Prof Veeramony. The son of a clerk, he was a self-made man, who had financed his studies by giving tuitions to juniors. After getting a job, he continued the tuitions to supplement his income. Even so, he respected students like me who did not seek tuitions. Prof Veeramony's booming voice resonated in the classroom. He was also a good singer and would render romantic Mohamed Rafi and Yesudas numbers with much feeling. Very handsome, he was admired by the girls in the college, yet seemed totally unaffected by all the attention.

He was, of course, a great teacher too. I have not come across another who could draw a perfect circle freehand on the blackboard. In geometry classes, he would draw, perfectly, all the figures given in the question. As he said, "Draw the perpendicular from P on AB", he'd hold the tip of the chalk and then you could hear a series of tic-tic-tic ... on the blackboard as a dotted line through P emerged at an exact right angle to AB. Voila! So, I waited for the next time he'd do it. It took me a fortnight's practice during lunch recess to come anywhere near his seemingly effortless feat.

Yet, after earning an MSc with all that maths, I spent my working life in banks. Minding other people's money was never on my wish-list. After all that hope and planning, I keep wondering if that was the tragedy of my life.

THE MARCONI MACHINE

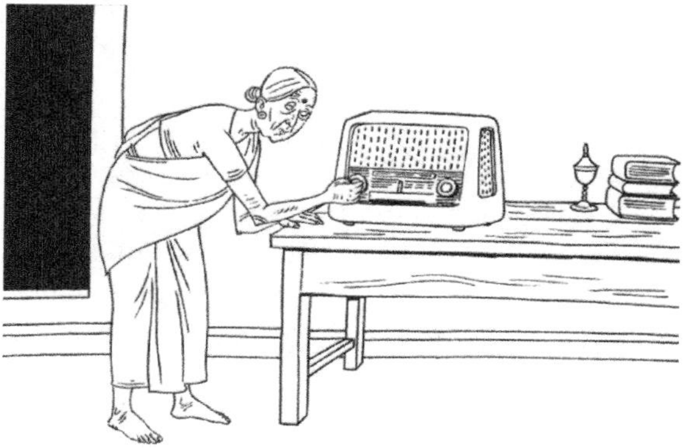

It was during a recent three-week holiday in Bengaluru with my son that I realised how addicted I was: Just four days in the Garden City, and I had already started missing my daily fix of Anantapuri FM, a Trivandrum radio channel.

The first thing I do every morning while at home in Trivandrum is to reach for the radio. And my Marconi Machine remains on as long as we are home. It's switched off only when we go out or at 11 pm when Kabban Mirza (or Nimmy or whoever) closes the station with the 'Aap ki Farmaaish' programme wishing the listeners a '*shubh raatri*', '*shabba khair*' or '*khudaa haafiz*'. (I might go to bed at 9:30, but the radio does so only at its designated time!)

Radio has been a habit with me for decades. I even bought a "transistor" with my first salary. It worked fine in Trivandrum, but in the rural areas I was posted to, the signals were weak. Unless one had nimble fingers that worked the tuning knob accurately, the radio would stay dumb or just emit static.

Our family's first radio was Achhamma's large Grundig. It had a perforated board behind through which I could peek at the valves (these were like glass bulbs with elements). After the radio was switched on, these valves slowly acquired a glow and, after about a minute, the loudspeaker would come alive, often with a crackle, and, if one was lucky, a human voice or the strains of instrumental music.

The Grundig worked on a cuboidal 12-volt battery pack made by Estrela (or was it Eveready?). As the battery was quite expensive, an inventive uncle of mine reduced the recurring cost by making a contraption that could accommodate eight 1.5-volt A-size cells. That was my first taste of Indian *jugaad* (innovative problem-solving)!

What also fascinated us kids was the radio's 'magic eye', a small glowing translucent plastic part its face. It helped monitor the tuning. As Achhamma (not many others were allowed to touch it) turned the tuning-knob gently, ever-so-gently, the static noise would fade and the magic eye, so far asleep, would acquire a soft glow. As she zeroed in on the station, the intensity of the static would fall further, to be overpowered by human voice or instrumental music. When the magic eye was at the greenest best, that was when she was bang on, we knew.

The All India Radio station nearest to Kannur, in North Malabar, where I spent most of my boyhood was Kozhikode, a good 60 miles away, and the schedule of programme was mostly in sync with the Trivandrum station. The signals were often not strong enough and at times, the magic eye would not glow at all, spreading gloom all around.

The heroes of medium wave (MW) then were giants in the literary firmament and theatre, like P Bhaskaran, Thikkodian, or Uroob, who had a significant role in shaping the aesthetic sensibilities of a few generations in Kerala. Trivandrum station had the likes of P Gangadharan Nair and T P Radhamony, whose voices enthralled listeners as much as the voice of their son Nanda Kumar does today.

Newsreaders Ramachandran and Rani (for quite some time, I had thought her name, thanks to her nasal accent, was Nani!) read Malayalam news from New Delhi. How can one forget the *'pravaachaka: Baladevaanandasaagarah'* of the *'yam aakaashavaani samprati vaartaaha shrooyantaam'*! That is the Sanskrit newsreader Baldev Anand Sagar gushing forth the equivalent of "This is Aahaashvaani. The news. Read by Baldev Anand Sagar."

On the English news scene, too, were several stalwarts: Melville DeMello, Surojit Sen and Barun Haldar updating us on the goings on in the country in their baritones.

Complementing (and competing with) them were the clear voices of Lotika Ratnam and Sphurti Sinha.

As a teenager, I used to listen to the BBC. Country Music USA from 7:00 to 7:30 am on the Voice of America was another delight. I'll never forget the sign-off line – "If you see someone without a smile, give him one of yours."

The Tamil Service of Radio Ceylon (now Sri Lanka Broadcasting Corporation, SLBC) was quite popular all over South India. An hour-long Malayalam programme anchored by a compere called, I think, Sarojini Shivalingam, aired in the evenings. Radio Ceylon's highlight was the Binaca Geet Mala at 8:00 pm on Wednesdays compered by the inimitable Ameen Sayani closely followed by *Aaj kaa Kalaakaar* and *Ek aur Anek*. He would rank and pack ten songs from new films into a fun-filled hour.

This monopoly of Radio Ceylon was broken when Vividh Bharati was launched in 1957. It offered several bouquets of Hindi film songs. Places like Jhumritalaiya and Rajnandgaon, hitherto unknown to the rest of India, became popular because of the listeners' choice programmes. Requests for songs were received from 'Yavatmal se Ramesh Bijapurkar, unki Shreemati Aarti, beta Bittoo, bitiya Sonali aur unke dher saare dost'. I wonder if some of these names were made up by the comperes themselves – as in 'Kandivli Mumbai se Kishore Kumar, Ashok Kumar, Nutan aur Mukesh', but who are we to deny some variety and fun to the Akashvani staff?

Perhaps as a matter of concession to South India, Vividh Bharati, most of whose programmes were in Hindi, broadcast 15 minutes each of Tamil, Malayalam, Telugu and Kannada songs from 4:30 to 5:30 pm, with the five-minute news bulletin at 5:00 eating into the quota for one of the languages. Vividh Bharati was fair and rotated the sequence every month, so that if it was Tamil that had only ten minutes last month, it would my Malayalam this month, Telugu the next and Kannada after that.

Transistor radios brought in a revolution. Portability was their selling point. One started to see people walking around or riding bicycles while listening to the radio. A lion's share of the credit for the popularity of cricket in India should, in my view, go to the transistor. The way cricket lovers strained their ears to listen to the live commentary needed to be seen to be believed. As one moved away from the 'range' of the radio station, one had to turn the aerial, the radio, or oneself in a direction that would enhance the quality of reception.

FM, mobile phones and internet radio have changed all that. Now music or news is on tap. You can store more music or podcasts in a tiny device and listen to it all your life. This easy availability has, I am afraid, taken away some of the charm of the music one coaxed out of grandmother's old Grundig.

THE SMELLS OF THE PAST

My friend Balachandran often lapses into nuanced writing. A keen and sensitive observer of the world around him, he is also, among other things, a brilliant photographer, nature-lover and blogger – all that despite having toiled, like me, in a bank for decades.

Recently, I returned to his blog after a long time. I was arrested by the truth concealed in three lines of his poem titled Old, Empty Bottles:

> Life, the elders would know,
> Is all about remembering the smells,
> The sights and sounds of the past.

Those lines sent me into a reverie – of the smells of the past. The earliest smell that I can remember is that of camphor. It was the smell I woke up to at dawn. Achhamma would burn a few slabs of camphor on a small bronze plate with a handle and do an *aarti* before the pictures of gods and goddesses in her *pooja* room, but that is not the smell that brings Achhamma back. After her bath before sunrise, she would tread stealthily into the room I, still an infant, would be sleeping in. She would then open the wooden box on four legs (that *kaalpetti,* as it was called in Malayalam, would at time double as a seat) to take out fresh clothes that had been crisp-dried in the sun and neatly folded away. The scent of the clothes, not any sounds, would wake me up. Smell, scientists say, can silently trigger emotional memories more than any of the other senses. The aroma of camphor still takes me back to my dear, long-departed grandmother.

So does the smell of paddy being boiled before dehusking, a major process in those days. Grandmother would supervise the workmen as they cleaned the *uruli,* a large flat bronze cookware, which was placed on three large laterite blocks, a permanent fixture in our backyard. Dried paddy would be measured out into it, water added, and a big fire lit under it. Dried coconut fronds, coconut shells, and firewood served as fuel. The smell wafting as the paddy got cooked wasn't pleasant but was surely distinctive.

When I visit a village, the smell of milk boiling in an earthen pot on a fire of dry coconut fronds is yet another smell that takes me back to my childhood. It is indeed a rare thing in these days of gas and induction heaters.

Mention summer, and I am reminded of the smell of burning cashew shells. This was how the kernels were extracted at home. When the nuts are set fire to, the oil secreted in the shell start oozing and catching fire. That is when the fire is doused, and the kernels knocked out of their shells. These charred-brown cashew kernels, believe me, are infinitely tastier than the branded and immaculately white factory-made variety you get in cans and pouches.

Another smell I cannot forget is that of burning coconut-oil-smeared frangipani flowers (also known as plumeria, and *chempakam* in Malayalam) – those five-petalled ones with the golden yellow centre. Why would anyone burn flowers? Young girls of North Malabar used to observe a nine-day festival called Pooram for fertility and for getting a 'good' husband. It involved inviting Kamadeva (the Indian Cupid) into the house. Frangipani had a major role in the festival.

Not all these smells can be regularly experienced any more, especially in the cities I have moved to. Yet, when they do, the memories they evoke are like a time machine that takes me back seven decades to my childhood

THE WORLD IN A PAPER BAG

Recently, when Bhawani placed the vegetables she had bought from the market on the kitchen platform, I noticed that they were wrapped in an old newspaper. They were not in the usual polythene bag. I 'de-creased' the paper carefully, took it to the dining table and started reading it.

Hari, my older son, teased me: "Is it a summary of the current week's headlines you are reading?" A normal human was not expected to waste time on such dead scraps of outdated paper.

Every day, I read my favourite newspaper, you could say, from the ear panels to the imprint line. No prioritization or skipping items. Still, I cannot resist the urge to read any scrap of printed paper that crosses my path. "From where did you pick up this habit?" my son asks.

The question transports me back sixty years when I was not yet ten years old. No daily newspaper ever reached our village. The only "daily" one had access to was the one in which the local grocer Moosa Hajee packed our provisions: usually half a Malayalam broadsheet artfully shaped into a cone and tied with a jute string.

The glossy magazine pages – especially those with pictures – were a bit of a rarity, Moosa Hajee reserving them for infrequent purchases of jeerakashala rice or dry fruits and spices.

When I was young, I used to collect each and every such paper that crossed our threshold. I would carefully spread them on the bench which I would straddle and pore over every word, be it a tender notice for drainage systems, a news bit, or a change-of-name notification. I would read it to the last syllable.

In fact, so enamoured was I of this exercise that I could not wait to reach home to get my daily fix: on my way back from the grocer, I would crane my neck at impossible angles to follow a sentence around the circular bends and little tucks at the bottom of the bundle's topography. Naturally, this was more challenging than the more leisurely reading of any riveting stuff in the comfort of our home.

The shopkeepers in the town nearby were more sophisticated: they used bags made of newspaper. This was much to my dislike because it could not be read straightaway. I had to dismantle it – and, trust me, this demands a lot of care – tearing slowly and carefully along the gum-line and using the tail-end of a teaspoon to pry a particularly stubborn section apart.

Riveting, did I say? Indeed. It was not always newspapers: when the contents were a small quantity of cumin seeds or mustard, it would be the leaves of a personal diary or a page of handwritten class notes on Baburnama, chemical equations or the parliamentary system. Larger quantities (garlic, jaggery or shallots) would come wrapped in leaves from the books of account of a local trader. Bulky items like rice, sugar or potatoes gave the bonanza – broad newspaper sheets that provided hours of reading pleasure!

There, of course, was the occasional fix of 'literature'. Two paragraphs of a short story, a poem in free verse, the climax of a novel minus the last three paragraphs – my imagination got plenty of exercise. It was through this medium that I was introduced to short stories and novels. This was how I started on a lifelong adventure with crossword puzzles too.

In those days of monitored reading (No FTV or Star Movies even of the PG variety), chastely brought up young men of my acquaintance even had their first vicarious carnal experiences via these packing materials, treasuring smoothed out half-pages of particular prettiness: pin-ups from Blitz or Current maybe, that they had procured in moments of rare luck. Such were the small thrills.

I must thank a paper bag for whatever I know of Indian literature. One day, the week's raw pulses had been put into a large paper bag made from not one, but one and a half pages of a reasonably recent edition of the Katha, which is where I read a particularly interesting bit of an Assamese story and was enthralled. I started subscribing to the magazine a few years later.

These days paper bags are not made of pages from diaries and personal letters (who writes diaries or letters any more?). Even pages from textbooks, ledgers, question papers, answer scripts, class notebooks and old bills only make rare appearances. If in my childhood, paper bags were made of old (and I mean really old) newspapers, these days I see bags made from last month's newspaper or merchandise wrapped in yesterday's Express or Manorama.

Such speed is a little unsettling. It robs the reader of that mellowed, smooth, vintage quality, which was the prime joy of reading paper bags. If the call to save the earth by discarding the polythene bag also restores the sublime joy of unravelling mysteries that only a piece of old paper can, wouldn't that be a great spin-off?

A HAT AND A BOAT

I'm pottering around the bedroom of my brother-in-law Ranjith's suburban apartment in Singapore when I spot a tan broad-brimmed suede hat on the wall. You know, the kind cowboys wear. I've never seen Ranjith sporting any headgear, nor is he known to be adventurous in matters sartorial.

My curiosity is stoked, but I can't ask him because he is not home. His daughter tells me that all she knows is that it has some childhood association.

That evening, Ranjith and I discuss the hat over chilled beer. He takes me back to when he was a Class III student in Calcutta and the day his parents took him and his sister to New Market for a bit of shopping. As they were leaving, Ranjith's eyes fell on a tan broad-brimmed hat with a red feather stuck to it.

"I imagined myself wearing it and riding a horse in the Wild West," Ranjith tells me, "and so I asked my mother to buy it, but she said No!" Ranjith then turned to his father. No luck again. He then did what many seven-year-olds in his situation do: screamed and threw a tantrum, refusing to budge unless he got the hat. But the parents ignored him and walked on. Ranjith stayed put, hoping that they would eventually return and give in.

"How wrong I was! They walked away briskly, dragging my sister along, without ever looking back," Ranjith recalls. They were nearly out of sight when Ranjith realized that his satyagraha was not yielding results. He gave up, but not before taking a pledge to buy a hat like that for himself someday.

All that reminded me of my boat. When I was a child of about that age, my father had taken us one evening to a big exhibition. There were potato-peelers and coconut-scrapers, egg-slicers and vegetable shredders, bedsheets and garments, saplings and grafted plants, and, of course, toys.

One stall had a shallow pit, about five feet in diameter, filled with water. Several tiny metal boats in bright colours were floating there, a few of them spluttering busily. On closer observation, I spotted in each of them a tiny sealed tank with tubes, a bowl with some oil and a burning wick in it.

I badly wanted one of them but was not bold enough to ask Achhan. I made a feeble representation to my mother, who told me why it wasn't right for me: children should not be playing with fire – or water, for that matter. The real reason, I now know, was that my strict father wasn't wasting hard-earned money on such trifles. I had to lump it.

Three decades later, I was with Bhawani and my little son Hari at a fair in Trivandrum. It had rained that evening. Dodging puddles with a shopping bag, an umbrella, and a four-year old in tow, is no easy proposition. So, we had to steer clear of several stalls where rainwater had collected.

As we walked past one such stall, I heard a splutter that triggered old memories. I turned back quickly, and before I knew it, I had bought it! I was out of the stall as fast as I had gone in. I could not wait to get home. I told Bhawani that I'd just bought a toy for Hari.

When we reached home, Hari was sleepy, but I was in a hurry to commission the boat. As Bhawani got busy in the kitchen, I filled the large plastic basin in the bathroom with water, placed the boat on the surface, poured a little oil in the bowl and lit the wick. The boat spluttered and moved. Hari's face lit up too.

After a week, my son seemed bored with it. Meanwhile, Bhawani, I didn't know, had been wondering why I was taking much longer than usual in the bath – until one Sunday when she caught me red-handed. Boating.

THE THRILLS OF THEYYAM

As the din gets more distinct, I can distinguish the resounding tribal rhythm of the drumbeat. The primaeval pulsations rising above the cacophony of the milling crowd is the first sign that we're nearing our destination. Unable to contain his excitement, my little son Gautam canters along, with me in tow. Our path is lit only by a few stars. I look up: the monsoon having receded, the sky is bereft of dark clouds. All this and rustle of dry leaves under our feet on the village mud-track sends me on a nostalgic trip. My thoughts go back to my schooldays.

I had written 'Theyyam' at the top of the page in large letters and underlined it. It was our Class Seven English composition period and Easow Master had given us 30 minutes to write an essay titled "When I grow up, I want to be a …".

"Why do I want to become a Theyyam?" I pondered the question. These oracles heard the grievances, anxieties and prayers of ordinary men and women, conveyed them to the gods and recommended "favourable considerations". People even thanked the gods by dropping offerings into their open palms. The only persons the Kaaranavar, the presiding head of our joint family, bowed to were the likes of Kunhappa and Ramunni, when they were in Theyyam garb. Even the Kaaranavar, who normally ordered people about, listened to them. A Theyyam seemed all-powerful.

Perhaps I was also enamoured by the mumbo-jumbo a Theyyam uttered, eyes turned heavenwards and hands outstretched. Perhaps because his unintelligible prophecies delivered with the quiver in his high-pitched voice, were awaited eagerly by the devout. A Theyyam seemed closer to the gods than my grandmother who regularly fasted and prayed. The Theyyam brought solace to men and women worried about their failed crops, the waywardness of their spouses or the illness of their offspring.

"The lights!" shrieks Gautam as we follow the curve in the road. Eager to reach there, he trots ahead of me. When I catch up, I too can see, in the general direction of our Tharawaad, a halo of lights in the sky. Theyyam – the word describes the oracle, his dance and the festival – would be performed in the courtyard of the complex.

The headquarters of the Tharawaad comprises three blocks of buildings constructed in different eras: a traditional single-storeyed *ettukettu*, a single-storeyed complex with two inner courtyards in the traditional style; a two-storeyed main building, which came later, seems to have been influenced by Dutch architecture and the third, called the *banglaav* (bungalow) resembles a clubhouse. It was built in the late 19th century, mainly to entertain British officials ruling Malabar, then part of Madras Presidency. The Kaaranavar liked to chat and tipple with friends there in the evenings.

Going ahead, you can see the Theyyam performers in different stages of preparation in the raised ground near the *kalari,* their performance arena. Some, having had their makeup done and dressed in Theyyam gear, are all set to make their appearance. Other Theyyams are waiting to dress up for later performances.

It's not only their colourful show or the sounds that accompany it that I take in. It is the smells of Theyyam. That of coconut oil as it is consumed by the flares, of turmeric, of arrack and beedis smoked, the scent of plantain leaf getting 'cooked' as piping hot rice is dropped on to it; the aroma of wooden logs as they turn into embers and then to ash as the fire, into which Ucchitta Bhagavati plunged herself, dies down.

There is a nip in the air, for it is the month of Makaram (January-end). Small groups of people are huddled together and watching the goings-on. Members of our family walk about with an affected demeanour: it-is-in-my-Tharawaad-that-this-event-is-taking-place kind of air of authority.

The smells and the sights of Theyyam haven't changed, I realize as I watch the spectacle with Gautam. The headgears worn by Theyyams representing the likes of Kantaakarnan are tall and heavy: the performers must strain to maintain their balance. Old-timers believe that, unhappy with the misdoings of us earthlings during the past year, the gods are disappointed. So, at one point, the Theyyams walk out of the kalari, where the gods they represent are believed to reside 363 days of the year. If they are to do their bidding, they might wreak havoc. Theyyams are all about grossly exaggerated legends or stories that reflect the man's fears – his defencelessness when confronted by floods, epidemics, snakes, wild beasts. So, to avert such natural fury, mortals placate the gods with offerings over the next two days. Adoring and appeasing the deities, they coax the Theyyams back into the kalari for another year. After these two days, it's life as usual and every Theyyam performer returns to his normal life – farm worker, kalari trainer, milkman or postman.

Theyyam used to be the only time the womenfolk of the village, who seldom ventured out, could get their stock of adornments and cosmetics – bangles, trinkets, surma (collyrium), local perfume and talcum powder, safety pins, hairclips, false hair, and such other things. Kids like me would cadge money out of uncles and dads to buy balloons, whistles, balls or assorted wooden toys. They came in all colours, shapes and sizes, and any amount of money you had was too little. It was our Christmas.

"Time's up!" Easow Master announced and sheets of paper began to rustle. I should have written all this, but I was so lost in thoughts about the festival, I didn't realize the half-hour had passed. All I could do was turn in my answer sheet with just the word THEYYAM on it.

MANIETTAN

When Maniettan died,he was barely 47.

He was my cousin, several times removed. If you ask me, we two were precariously perched somewhere on the family tree. We knew we were cousins only because our families had lived in the same village for generations.

More than cousins, we were friends, although Maniettan was a good fifteen years older. He taught biology in the the family-run high school. His other interests lay in literature, music, puzzles, riddles.

When I was in the primary school, he would spend weekends with us. My uncle and he went to the same college and they spent holidays together for what they termed “combined study”. Maniettan would spend a lot of time with me. He would make me list the names of my classmates. And I would oblige: Abbas, Aravindan, Bharati, Bhaskaran, Chandran, Damodaran, Ebrahim, Geeta, Govindan, … till Yashoda, Zubair and Zuhara.

Then he would ask me to list them in the order they sat in class, which was: Parthan, Mohamed, Chandran, … Hari and Abbas, followed by Jameela, Yashoda, Leela, Janaki, … and Kalyani. It was not until I grew up that I realized that all was his home-grown method aimed at sharpening my memory.

Maniettan would make me recite the multiplication tables. When I nearly reached the end, like thirteen sevens make ninety-one, he would pretend that I had made a mistake and challenge me: “Thirteen sevens make …?” And I would have to recite the whole table all over again – his method of making sure that I memorised the tables even better.

Maniettan also wrote poems and short stories. He had a baritone voice and would sing Saigal numbers in his characteristic style. His rendition of “*Suhana safar aur yeh mausam haseen*” on the mouth organ had enlivened many a night I had spent with him.

It was much later, after he started out as a teacher in our school that I came to know his official name: Vipin Chandran. The school was Maniettan’s passion. He was a natural leader and a great organizer too. A couple of months after he joined the school as a teacher, he mobilized the senior students during the Onam holidays to exhume the skeleton of the temple tusker which had been buried some years earlier. Holes were drilled through the bones, which were then joined together using thick copper wire. The elephant skeleton still occupies a central place in the school's biology lab.

With his penchant for science exhibitions, Maniettan led the school team to State-level expos. He coaxed the management to cough up tidy sums every year to hold annual science exhibitions in the school. Under his guidance, the students made working models of drip irrigation, biogas plants and the like. All this did not go unrecognized: he was decorated with the Best Teacher awards in Kerala and South India.

In his devotion to the school and his profession and in the pursuit of his passions, he seems to have somehow neglected his health. He smoked and drank a lot. When elders said all that was a bad influence on the young, he brushed it off laughing, "They had said that about Socrates too."

It was Maniettan he who lit my first cigarette. It was he who poured me my first drink. It was he also he who stoked my interests in literature, puzzles, music. Maybe even gave me a memory that helps me recall all these details six decades later, today. He showed me a world outside the school and helped make me what I am.

But, as for Maniettan himself, he left at 47, when he should have been at the prime of his life.

T

THE NATURE CLUB

Though officially he was Vipin Chandran, the science teacher in our school in the village was Mani Ma'sh to students and Maniettan to everybody else. An enterprising man, he believed in inculcating scientific temper in children and sensitizing his students about nature and ecology, long before environment and biodiversity had become buzzwords. He had novel ideas to make even the drabbest subject appealing. Rather than rely on textbook illustrations, he would ask us to bring in live specimens of plants and insects. It wasn't for nothing that his peers thought him to be a bit odd.

So, displays got added at no cost to what was an apology for a school laboratory until Vipin Chandran Master's arrival. He had given standing orders to his students that the news of any snake having been killed should be reported to him. Be it the dead of night or thunderstorm, he would rush there with a glass jar of formaldehyde and return with a prized addition to the school's biology laboratory.He would take his students on treks in the nearby hills and forests, where they would see for themselves live specimens of aerial roots, alternate leaf arrangements, various fruits, chameleons, warblers, weaverbirds, nature's camouflages. A tailorbird's nest, dried leaves and flowers of every description mounted on cardboard – all came in handy.

At one point, it occurred to him that the awareness of the students could be further kindled if they'd set up a Nature Club. The children were awash with ideas: they could go to the wooded areas and collect samples of flowers and leaves, or to the riverside and identify fish species. They could even trek to hilly Tirunelli during the Onam holidays to observe its diverse flora and the fauna.

There was one problem, however. These projects needed funds. The idea would not get past the headmaster, who had always thought of the science buff as an eccentric and his ideas too newfangled. Even if the headmaster okayed it, there was little chance of getting financial support from the school's skinflint of a manager.

One of the boys suggested that funds be mobilized through a collection drive. Some teachers contributed their mite. Children chipped in with small change, but all that added up to too small a sum for any Nature Club's needs.

Perhaps the locality's affluent people would be touched by the idea, someone said. After all, it was a very good cause, was it not? So, off they went, to Kumaran Vydyar, who ran his thriving Ayurveda clinic, Sankaran Namboodiri the landlord and 'Vyaghram' Subbu Iyer the local moneylender, among others. Though all of them were not equally forthcoming, the response was positive.

One person approached was Mammu Hajee, a trader in cash crops. Barely literate though he was, good causes brought out his benevolence.

The leader of the group of students briefly explained their mission to the affluent Hajee – all about the founding of a Nature Club in the school which would meet on the first Monday of every month. Not one to shirk his responsibility to society, the Hajee fished into one of the pockets of the broad green-and-red belt that held his chequered lungi and his corpulent person together, extracted a 1000-rupee note, and thrust it into the leader's hands, saying, "Why stop with a mere *neychore* (ghee-rice) club? You youngsters should eat well. Set up a Biriyani Club which can meet every Friday!"

THREE DEAR UMMAS

Our house in the village had an annexe of sorts. It was really a dark, musty, ill-ventilated room surrounded by large verandahs. The room, always locked, was used for storing agricultural produce like cashew, pepper, arecanut or coconut. While the verandah on the west was used for storing firewood, the one on the north was where the cattle were often sheltered. The other two verandahs served many ends: that was where the women household help took rest and chatted. Part of it was a work area, where vegetables were diced, and rice was ground into idli or appam batter.

Whenever I remember the annexe, three women come to mind: Kadeesumma, Ayisumma and Mariyumma. For Kerala Muslims, Umma means mother. When used as a suffix to a name, it is a mark of respect.. They were among the many hangers-on that my maternal grandmother had, but even as a five-year-old, I could see that they were very different from the rest. While all the other women wore printed blouses in solid colours and white mundus with thin borders, these three were in long-sleeved embroidered blouse-tops made of thin white fabric. They also covered the lower half of their body with a *kaachimundu*, a mundu with a broad two-toned border in bold purple, green, violet or blue. They also adorned large earrings, nose-rings, anklets and rings on their fingers and toes – all this in silver. Around their slender wrists were glass bangles in a myriad of colours.

Kadeesumma and Mariyumma were sisters and Ayisumma was Kadeesumma's only daughter, but the three women were very different from each other. The short, dark Mariyumma, then in her early forties, was the oldest. Kadeesumma, a bit younger, was tall and fair. Ayisumma, around 20, was stunningly pretty. The three lived an impoverished life, with no men in their little thatched house. The childless Mariyumma's wayward husband had long left her. Kadeesumma's husband, who ran a small shop, had died of malaria. Nobody could fathom why, but the *nikaah* of young Ayisumma, too, was short-lived.

While the other hangers-on – like Deviamma and Maathuamma – helped in our kitchen and did other tasks within the house, the three Ummas never entered the main house. Most days, they were assigned odd jobs like watering the plants, collecting cashews, clearing the compound or steaming paddy in the annexe.

All three Ummas would report before nine in the morning and work till 4 pm. The days were hectic for them when Kunhiraman came to crop coconuts. Repeated eight times in a year, each cropping was a three-day affair because our compound was large. The Ummas would gather the coconuts and pile them in the front yard. It then took a few more busy days to collect and clear the compound of the fronds and the other debris cut from the treetops.

All three worked hard for a living. At their own home, they reared goats and a brood of hens. Their day began early when they collected eggs and milked the goats. They would sell the eggs and milk in the village. Every Saturday morning, Ayisumma would come with a clutch of eggs for an uncle who worked in the town and would be home for the weekend, a concession he had wrested from Achhamma, who had ran our otherwise strictly vegetarian household.

Like all the others, the Ummas were paid in kind: with paddy or rice. To me, they seemed a happy lot despite their poverty and all their toiling. They would sing as they pounded rice and talk animatedly while clearing weeds in our compound.

We children looked forward to *Ramzan* festival because the Ummas, decked in their finery, would arrive with a hamper of dates, dry fruits and other goodies that we rarely saw. Achhamma would accept the delicacies after confirming once again that the stuff was purely vegetarian.

We loved the Ummas for another reason too: in the summer, their day's work was done, they would light a small fire and roast some cashewnuts, shell them and give us the kernels. They tasted just divine, I tell you!

The Ummas had a special place in Achhamma's heart too. She had allowed them some unusual perks: the rice bran for their hens, jackfruit-tree leaves for the goats and enough coconut fronds to re-thatch their little house, an annual exercise in the summer, before the monsoons.

One evening, as the Ummas were leaving, Maathuamma, who was bringing back the cows from the fields, noticed that the corners of the kaachimundu the three Ummas wore had been tied into knots, each with about a handful of rice, Maathuamma suspected. She promptly reported this to Achhamma, adding for good measure that the few coconuts found behind a bush, in an area supposed to have been cleared by the Ummas a couple of days back, must have been hidden away by them to smuggle out later.

Achhamma brushed all that aside. "Maathuamma, you must be imagining things!" I heard Achhamma say, "when the coconuts were cropped, a few must have rolled off into the bushes."

Even if those allegations were true, Achhamma understood. And we all got lesson in kindness that day. After Maathuamma left, I heard Achhamma telling my mother, "God only knows, life for the poor Ummas must be so hard. A fistful of rice and a few coconuts can mean a lot to them."

A MAN OF LETTERS

During a vacation in my village years back, I ran into Daamuettan, the postman. Shrivelled and shrunk, he was still trudging long distances to deliver the mail. I'd imagined he had long retired, for he was a postman even in my youth, which makes it well over forty-five years of service! When I asked him about superannuation, Daamuettan shrugged his shoulders and said, "I can push a couple of years more; we extra-departmental postmen have no retirement."

A genial soul, he was (and still is) Daamuettan to every man or woman, old and young. He had started work as a peon in our elementary school and doubled as a postman

– quite like his boss Balan Master, our schoolteacher who moonlighted as the postmaster.

Daamuettan had set his own practices and rules for mail delivery. The first batch of delivery was at the point of origin – the post office itself. A small crowd would be waiting there every evening for the private bus named "Jayashree" to arrive with the mail bag. Daamuettan would open the bag, separate the special mail (things like registered letters and money orders) for the postmaster's scrutiny. Then ... thud, thud, he would affix the delivery stamp on each of the remaining items – one thud on the stamp pad and another on the letter.

As the thuds resound rhythmically, the expectant crowd outside would swell in size. He would read aloud the names above the addressees of the missives, and those present there would come forward and collect them. People were free to collect letters meant for their neighbours too.

A vigilant observer could notice a pattern he followed while putting away the letters that could not be disposed of at this point: they were sorted into a few small heaps – geographically, one presumed.

Daamuettan would first head for the banyan tree in front of the Krishna temple, where people would assemble in the evening to exchange the hottest gossip, play cards or just hang about. Delivering the first bunch of letters there would mean emptying about half the contents of his bag.

The roving delivery would start the next morning. Other things being equal, he gave priority to money orders and registered letters. He knew that aged parents might be looking forward to remittances from their employed children and youngsters would be awaiting call letters for interviews and appointment orders. The small tip that recipients of these items gave him was incidental, but incentive enough.

Book posts and newspapers (yes, they used to arrive by post!) received the lowest priority in Daamuettan's scheme of things. These would be held over till some "regular" mail came for the same addressee – or a neighbour. I often saw three or four issues of the Indian Express delivered to my uncle in a bunch.

Most of the letters in those days were postcards because, it seems, in the trade-off between privacy and frugality, the latter won hands down. As Daamuettan walked through the fields and through the lanes, he would glance at the letters. So, while delivering the letters, he would also announce, "Karthiyedathi, nothing to worry, Raghavettan has reached NEFA safely" or "Kanaetta, your granddaughter has lost a milk tooth." The recipients would not take offence at his having had a sneak preview of the postcard before they could see it.

Even in Kerala, not many were literate in those days. But help was always at hand in the form of Daamuettan. At times, his assistance would be sought even for writing out replies – something he happily did. This role of reader-cum-scribe would have made Daamuettan privy to the secrets of several families. To give the devil his due, some professional ethics still ruled. Daamuettan would never reveal to others any such bit he'd read.

Daamuettan remained an institution. He had a share in the joys and the sorrows of every family in the village. He rejoiced when Appukkuttan got an appointment order, he was crestfallen when he brought the news that the right leg of Kumaran Nair, the jawan, was blown off when he stepped on a mine.

However, for me, there remains an enigma. It is one thing to read a postcard, but how on earth could he at times know the contents of sealed inland letters and envelopes? I recall one evening during a summer vacation, Daamuettan brought an envelope to our neighbour. "Santhedathi has missed her periods again," he said while handing it over to the lady of the house. "You must ask her to stop, Kalyani Amma. This would be her seventh child, right?"

MALABAR'S FRENCH CONNECTION

In recent years, the exclamatory word "Aiyoh!" widely used in South Indian languages, made it to the Oxford English Dictionary. Not so the exclamation "Oui!", popular in North Malabar.

Unlike in French, "Oui!" in Malabar is actually a variant of "Oosh!", often employed for expressing disgust – or annoyance – as in *"Oosh... entoru chood!"* meaning "Oh, it's so hot here!" At times, oui is used in conjunction with other words, like *"Oui, ente daivame!"* (Oh, my God!).

Intoned appropriately, the Malabari oui is in fact a versatile exclamation used to express surprise, pleasure, fear, pain, bashfulness, sorrow.

Anyone with a smattering of French would know that the word has an altogether different meaning in France. It simply means Yes. Like, if asked *"Du café?"* ("Some coffee for you?"), and you like the idea, you'd answer, *"Oui ..."*

So, enough of semantics and comparative linguistics.
Let's get to the point.

If you have lived for a while in Tellicherry or Kannur in Malabar, you would certainly have noticed the French influence there, particularly in the district of Mahé, starting with that acute-accented é. As in France, roads have names starting with Rue, schools are l'écoles, as authentically portrayed by M Mukundan in his Malayalam novel *Mayyazhippuzhayude TheeranngaLil,* for instance. You would also have noticed that there are local people who stand out from the general dusky, Dravidian crowd. Tall and fair, these outliers are endowed with distinctly European features.

But oui, what's this French connection? Let me go by what an older cousin of mine once told me.

All of us know how, centuries ago, foreigners – the Portuguese, the French, the Dutch, among others, attracted by the scent of pepper and other spices had headed for the Malabar coast and of how the British East

India Company started to colonise us. As for the French, the places where they established strongholds – like Chandernagore, Pondicherry, Karaikal and Yanam – included Mahé.

It is believed that the name Mahé was given in honour of Bertrand François Mahé de la Bourdonnais (1699 - 1753). There is also a claim that the spelling Mahé was officially adopted by the leader of the expedition that retook the city in 1726 in recognition of La Bourdonnais' role. But original French documents from the early 1720s refer to Mayé, also spelt Mahé and Mahié, have given lie to those theories. Scholars have concluded that Mahé derives from Mayyazhi, the Malayalam name for the local river and region.

And, my cousin went on, the French had built barracks for their soldiers on the elevated plains nears the banks of the Mayyazhi. In front of the barracks was the huge *maidan,* which doubled as the parade ground. If a soldier in the barracks looked out of the windows, he'd see verdant meadows on the other bank, cows grazing, farmers with their bullocks, women with headloads of harvested paddy.

The denizens of these barracks – well-built, muscular, tall and fair-complexioned – were a novelty to the locals. From afar, they would watch the soldiers with interest as they marched and exercised on the maidan.

As for the soldiers, they found the humid coastal weather oppressive and not knowing any Malayalam, they would have felt the absence of any social life.

The sight one of them saw, the story goes, when he looked out through the high window one morning was a treat: a bevy of carefree village belles walking along the riverbank. They were going for a bath at a favoured spot by the river. He called his mates and shared the spectacle.

For the soldiers starved of female company, this was something. Their daily schedule now had a new item: waiting for the girls on their way to their hour-long bath and back. Unseen by the girls, this went on for some time until one irrepressible soldier whistled out loud as the girls gamboled, swam and splashed about in the river. They turned and looked but found nothing. The men would have ducked, and little did the girls expect the men to be peeping.

Another day, some of the men came out to watch. As the girls walked along the swampy riverbank past the barracks, one of the soldiers said something out loud to them. History does not record what the exact words were, but from the attendant circumstances, we can conjecture that it must have been something romantic, and in French.

The girls turned and saw half a dozen young men waving at them.

The bashful girls scurried past, crying *"Oui! Oui!"*

The rest, as they say, is history. French blood mixed easily with Dravidian blood. Born was a whole new brood of tall, fair, good-looking men – and beautiful women – with auburn hair and distinctly French features who all speak Malayalam.

DEBT-FREE FIRST

North Malabar of the 1920s. Koodaali, where I grew up, and Kallyaad, another small village, were about twelve miles – 19 kilometres – apart and the only way to get from one place to the other then was by foot. A gang of thugs frequented the route and were particularly active between dusk and dawn. So, solitary travellers, even small groups, avoided the route during these hours.

Daamu and Kelu, cousins of about the same age, were from Koodaali. They even got married around the same time. Their wives too were cousins from Kallyaad. But the similarities ended there.

Daamu was a schoolteacher. Contrary to custom, Daamu didn't move to his wife's home. He continued stay in Koodaali since it was much closer than Kallyaad to his school. He would only spend the weekends at his wife's place. Kelu was in business. He would buy coconut, arecanut, pepper, cashew and other produce to sell in the nearby town's market.

Like other such businessmen, he operated by offering a token advance to have a lien on a year's crop in a coconut grove or on all the pepper in a plot, maybe even the right to a season's cashew crop. That meant they'd be expected to pay the contracted amount in bits and pieces by the end of the year. But, often, some typical excuse would be offered for not paying up: poor crop quality, the yield was far lower than expected, the rains came too soon, the summer was too severe and too many tender coconuts dropped off prematurely. This way, they would normally get away by paying no more than three-fourths of the amounts agreed to.

Schoolmaster Daamu had inherited some land and the savings from his salary helped him acquire more land. One year, the story went, Kelu offered an advance to Daamu for his coconut crop. A firm believer in the dictum that doing business with a loved one could harm the relationship, Daamu had other plans: he would deal with Mammu Hajee, another local businessman. "If the full amount is not paid to me," Daamu explained to Kelu, "I can quarrel with Mammu. Can I do that with you?"

Even so, Kelu was insistent. And when some elders in their extended family intervened, Daamu had to relent, finally arriving at a mutually acceptable solution. The cost was reduced, but the full amount, Rs 50 – a tidy sum in those days – would be paid by Kelu in advance.

Alas, when the day of reckoning came, Kelu said he was short of money: he had only Rs 40 to spare, but he assured his dear cousin that the remaining Rs 10 would be paid before the Onam festival, when people like him usually have more cash. That sounded reasonable and Daamu agreed.

Then, one Friday evening, Daamu was walking to his wife's village for the weekend. There was a lurking fear in his mind: the thugs. Still, he mustered courage and quickened his pace. A couple of miles on, he saw the figure of another man ahead of him. If he could catch up, Daamu thought, two men would be more formidable than his lone self. So, he walked even faster and soon caught up with the other man only to realise that it was none other than Kelu. Kelu was also on his way to Kallyaad to his wife's place, after his day at the market.

As they walked along chatting, each one secretly hoped they would not encounter the notorious thugs. Yet, neither of them discussed such things because they knew such a fear could be contagious.

Just then, three hefty men, moustachioed and menacing, loomed large before them. There was no escape, the two cousins realised.

"Remove your rings!" one thug ordered, while the other two grabbed the victims to ensure they would not flee.

Daamu and Kelu rid their fingers of their solid gold wedding rings.

"Out with the money!" was the next command.

While the schoolteacher fished around his bag for small notes and loose change, Kelu took some cash from the folds of his mundu around his waist and thrust it into Daamu's hand: "Here's the ten I owe you!"

GOODBYE, HIGH SCHOOL!

It was with a tinge of sadness that I heard it: a ritzy multi-storeyed commercial complex was to replace my alma mater. I'd spent the last two years of high school there. It was no Sherwood, Doon or Mayo, it was plain old HEHMMHS.

Located bang in the middle of the bustling Mattancherry market, **H**ajee **E**ssa **H**ajee **M**oosa **M**emorial **H**igh **S**chool, named after its benevolent founder, was far from being one of Kochi's top-of-the-shelf schools. It was a poor cousin of the neighbouring Gujarati Vidyalaya and the Tirumala Devaswom High School, both run by wealthy trusts.

The upkeep of the imposing two-storey building was never a priority. The heirs of the founder perhaps had other needs or fallen into bad times. Starved of resources, its students were left to fend for themselves, especially during the periods set aside for drawing, craft, sports and games or physical training.

Our teachers went to great lengths in their efforts to instruct students. There was no laboratory but there was creativity. Mr Subramanian, the chemistry teacher, would hold a piece of chalk vertically and say "Suppose you take this test tube ...", then point to some chalk powder and say, "and put some potassium chlorate into it ...", and bringing his other fist, supposed to represent the spirit lamp, below the chalk, add, "… and heat the test tube," he would go on, "oxygen will escape."

All my HEHMMHS teachers were a dedicated lot. Mrs Thressiamma loved physics so much, she gave extra classes on Sundays, undeterred by the low attendance even on regular days. Though you could get your SSLC those days even without pass marks in Hindi, our teacher Mr Namboodiri would pour his lungs out. Pranksters, looking for some diversion, would request him to explain the meaning of Bollywood film lyrics like *Dil-e-naadaan, tujhe hua kya hai…* or *Zindagi pyaar ki do-chaar ghadi hoti hai…,* and he would oblige, ever so patiently.

The khadi-clad Mr Wenceslaus (Venchappan to colleagues), who was also a municipal councillor, taught us English; the mathematics teacher Mr Govindankutty also ran the school's bookstore; the stern Mr Joseph's cane may have taught us more than his history lessons; Mr Sadanandan, a rationalist and a brilliant speaker, was the Malayalam teacher, but he could handle any subject for any class; the ageless Arabic teacher Munshi Syed, with his neatly trimmed grey beard, looked upwards of 60, but claimed to be in his late forties. And there was the reticent Headmaster Mr Mohamed Ali – it was a great team.

Though handicapped due to lack of funds, the school did very well in extra-curricular activities like the youth festivals and inter-school sports. In fact, HEHMMHS posed an effective threat to all the "good" schools in the district at such events.

The physical demise of the school, I am told, was the result of its lack of maintenance. Yet, in reality, over the years, it must have it failed to attract students – parents would have shunned the school because it did not produce results: once, in the 1970s, it had the dubious distinction of drawing a blank at the SSLC examination. Everybody failed.

So, if anyone who has been moderately successful in life reveals himself as HEHMMHS alumnus, you can bet he would be asked, in disbelief, "How come? Don't tell me you studied there!" I should know.

The tall, spiffy commercial complex rising from my school's debris at the junction of Kochi's New Road and Palace Road may be a sign of the times – commerce taking precedence over education. Yet, the spirit of my chemistry teacher with his make-believe spirit lamp or our good English King Wenceslas who taught this foreign language, will always reign there.

My passing from our school was a joyous occasion. So different is the passing of the school. Fortunately, the memories live on and no skyscraper can replace our days in the sun at HEHMMHS.

EPILOGUE

The tiny hamlet of Koodaali is no longer what it was. Though it is no Pall Mall or Madison Square, it has also yielded to the relentless changes that Time brings about on places. As you pass by, your smartphone detects dozens of wifi connections and the chances that your movements have not been recorded by a CCTV camera are slender. There is a bank branch, an ATM, a petrol station and a mall. It boasts of a private lying-in hospital and a shopping complex where you can buy practically anything.

So, if I were to tell someone that it was once a part of a remote countryside untouched by the trappings of what goes by the expression "modern conveniences, it is more likely that my credibility, if not my sanity, would be a subject of debate. The Koodaali that I spent my childhood in now exists only the memory of my contemporaries and seniors. I thought I owe it to the next generation to freeze them as they were and preserve them for whatever they are worth.

This small volume is the result of that thought.

Printed in Great Britain
by Amazon

42661141R00096